MASTER CLASS

A Comprehensive Improvisation Method
by Joe Elliott

Contents

Page   CD Track

Page	CD Track		
2			Introduction
4	1–2	**Chapter 1:**	Getting Started
6	3	**Chapter 2:**	Organizing Arpeggios in Major Scale Patterns
9	4	**Chapter 3:**	Organizing Arpeggios in Minor Scale Patterns
12	5	**Chapter 4:**	Situation Playing
15	6–9	**Chapter 5:**	The Connecting Game
19		**Chapter 6:**	The Connecting Game in More Patterns
21	10–13	**Chapter 7:**	Expanding Note Options with Added Color Tones
26	14	**Chapter 8:**	Introducing the Melodic Minor Scale
28	15	**Chapter 9:**	Adding Altered Tones
33		**Chapter 10:**	Referencing and Worksheets
36	16–19	**Chapter 11:**	The Connecting Game with the Altered Scale
40	20–21	**Chapter 12:**	The Locrian #2 Scale
43	22–25	**Chapter 13:**	Writing Licks
48	26–27	**Chapter 14:**	Inserting Licks
50	28–29	**Chapter 15:**	Disguising Licks
53	30	**Chapter 16:**	Harmonizing the Melodic Minor Scale for Altered Dominants
58	31	**Chapter 17:**	Harmonizing the Melodic Minor Scale for Minor 7(♭5) Chords
62	32–33	**Chapter 18:**	Turnaround Licks in Major (III–VI–II–V–I)
67	34–35	**Chapter 19:**	Turnaround Licks in Minor (I–VI–II–V–I)
72	36–39	**Chapter 20:**	The Lydian ♭7 Scale
75	40–41	**Chapter 21:**	Harmonizing the Melodic Minor Scale for Non-Functioning Dominants
78	42–43	**Chapter 22:**	Non-Resolving II–V Progressions
83	44–50	**Chapter 23:**	The Bebop Bridge
88	51–53	**Chapter 24:**	Chromatic Connections
91	54–65	**Chapter 25:**	Other Melodic Devices
95		**Chapter 26:**	Putting It Together
98		**Chapter 27:**	Solo Shaping
101		**Chapter 28:**	How to Budget Practice Time
103			Conclusion

ISBN 978-0-634-00970-9

7777 W. BLUEMOUND RD. P.O. BOX 13819 MILWAUKEE, WI 53213

In Australia Contact:
Hal Leonard Australia Pty. Ltd.
4 Lentara Court
Cheltenham, Victoria, 3192 Australia
Email: ausadmin@halleonard.com.au

Copyright © 2008 by HAL LEONARD CORPORATION
International Copyright Secured All Rights Reserved

No part of this publication may be reproduced in any form or by any means without the prior written permission of the Publisher.

Visit Hal Leonard Online at
www.halleonard.com

Introduction

If you're like me, your first experience playing a guitar solo was in your friend's basement or garage. You probably learned the A minor pentatonic scale in fifth position, learned a few repetitive "didlee-diddles," a couple of bends, and had a great time jammin'. When I figured out what key a song was in, I would move my minor pentatonic shape, didlee-diddles, and bends to the place on the neck that seemed to fit and—jam. The soloist in me didn't really seem to care that I didn't know too much.

Well, this was how I played for quite some time. I gradually expanded my knowledge by learning more patterns of minor and major pentatonic scales. I played with this amount of scale knowledge until I got into college and was introduced to some jazz guys. Playing tunes with them, I continued this basic approach but had to adapt to the songs changing keys more often. My solo approach, however, was still basically the same: figure out the key and wander around the pattern hoping I'd get lucky and play something good. This is called *key center soloing*, and there is nothing wrong with it. It's a wonderful way for us to break into the world of soloing early on in our musical development. It's great that we guitarists can learn to make good music with a small amount of information. But I knew there had to be more.

Most guitarists live in this stage of development for a long time with a growing sense that they are missing some important element that would make them sound better. They're right. What's missing is the knowledge of how to make your solo fit the chords the band is playing. How do the great players pick those great notes in their solos? Some people might refer to these notes as "sweet notes," but they are really just *chord tones*. Chord tones are simply the notes of the chord that the band is playing. This very simple concept, which is called *chord tone soloing*, is the basis for the technical side of playing jazz. The vehicle for playing chord tones is the arpeggio. Understanding the concept is simple; implementing it requires some special and organized efforts. This book is designed to do just that: organize and gradually build your fretboard knowledge to a level where chord tone playing becomes as natural as wandering around the minor pentatonic scale.

This book is based on the jazz improvisation method I've taught at G.I.T. since 1988. It works for the seasoned rocker who is ready for a new challenge or the jazz newcomer looking for a good start. The essence of the book can be summarized by the following statement.

As a developing player, you have two simple goals:
- To acquire a *vocabulary* (licks you know)
- To acquire a *repertoire* (songs you know)
  (For a song to be "in your repertoire" you must be able to play the melody, improvise a solo, and comp for another soloist—all from memory.)

This book will cover the following general topics to help you develop vocabulary:
- key center soloing
- chord tone playing
- arpeggios
- organizing arpeggios
- situation playing—the concept of extracting common chord progression fragments from tunes and learning vocabulary to play over them
- colorful note options
- writing licks (developing vocabulary)
- inserting the licks into songs
- acquiring and developing repertoire
- other melodic devices
- solo shaping

The book teaches a logical and systematic approach to learning to play over changes. Each chapter begins with a list of objectives that let you know what to keep your eye out for and what you should be learning. Related definitions of important musical terms are also included in several chapters. A summary appears at the end of each chapter as well, reiterating the important points covered to help make sure you haven't missed any vital information. Before you begin working through this book, I suggest that you read through chapters 26, 27, 28, and the conclusion. By doing this, all the work in the first 25 chapters will be more meaningful.

Prerequisites:

In order to receive the maximum benefit from the method this book teaches, you will need to know the following information:

1. **The harmonized major scale** – In other words, you must know that in a major tonality the I chord is ma7, II chord is mi7, III chord is mi7, IV chord is ma7, V chord is dom7, VI chord is mi7, and the VII chord is mi7(♭5).

2. **The harmonized minor scale** – In other words, you must know that in a minor tonality the I chord is mi7, II chord is mi7(♭5), ♭III chord is ma7, IV chord is mi7, the V chord is mi7 (but usually changed to dom7 in jazz), the ♭VI chord is ma7, and the ♭VII chord is dom7.

3. **At least Pattern I of the following major scale shapes:**

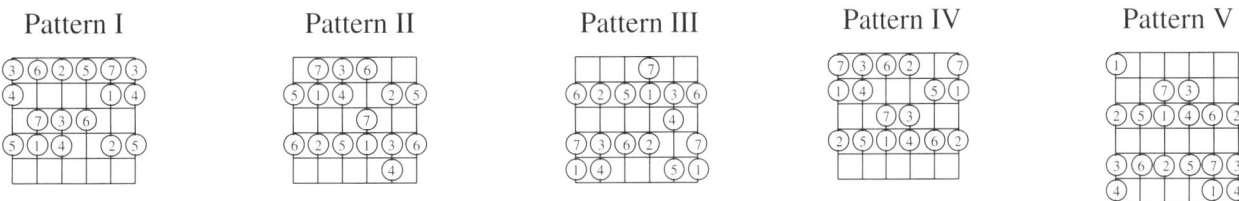

4. **At least Pattern II of the following minor scale shapes:**

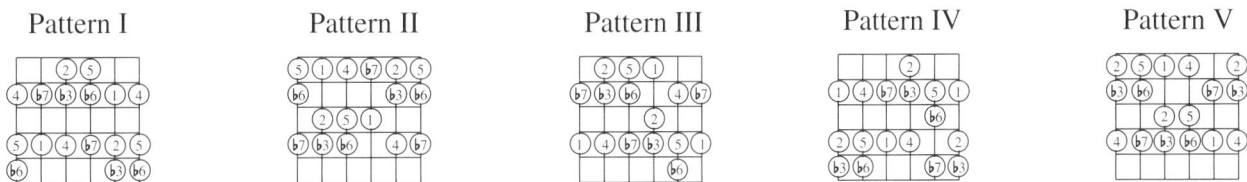

5. **You'll need to be a key center soloist or at least have a good grasp of the concept.**

6. **You'll need to know what an arpeggio is (but not necessarily how to play them).**

7. **You'll need to understand what the word "diatonic" means.**

8. **You'll need to know the seven diatonic modes and their related chord qualities:**
   Ionian = Major 7, Dorian = Minor 7, Phrygian = Minor 7, Lydian = Major 7,
   Mixolydian = Dominant 7, Aeolian = Minor 7, Locrian = Minor 7 (♭5).

Getting Started

1

> **Objectives:**
>
> - To understand key center soloing.
> - To understand how to change keys while key center soloing.
> - To understand what an arpeggio is.
> - To understand chord tone soloing.
>
> **Definitions:**
>
> - **Position** – determined by the fret number where your first finger is placed.
> - **Key Center Solo** – a solo where all the notes come from the scale of the song's key.
> - **Chord Tone Solo** – a solo where the notes include the specific tones of each chord the band is playing underneath the solo.
> - **Arpeggio** – a melodic device where the tones of a chord are played in succession rather than simultaneously.
> - **Chord Scale** – a scale that has a specific chord application. Usually a chord scale contains all the tones of the chord over which it will be used.

Key Center Soloing

Most guitarists will look at a chord progression like this one and figure out in what key it is written. Next, they'll find their favorite scale pattern and start making things up, wandering around the scale hoping they play notes and ideas that sound good.

Try this progression in the key of A minor. Solo from the A minor pentatonic scale in fifth position.

Track 1
(0:45)

In this progression Ami7 is the I chord, Dmi7 is the IV chord, and G7 is the ♭VII chord.

If you have a multi-track recorder to use, record yourself playing the chords on track 1 (or record the CD example onto track 1), and record yourself soloing on track 2.

Listen to your solo with the rhythm track. It probably sounds OK. Now, rewind and mute track 1 (the rhythm guitar track or CD example). Listen to the solo you just recorded without the rhythm track. If you can "hear" the notes of the chords being played in your solo, you either have great instincts or are very lucky. Most of us won't sound that good. We will sound like we're wandering aimlessly through the scale. You have just a played a key center solo.

Now try this. The next progression starts out like the last one but changes keys part way through. The first four measures are in the key of A minor, but the next three measures are in the key of E♭ major. Use the A minor pentatonic scale for the first four measures, the E♭ major pentatonic scale for the next three measures, and move back to A minor pentatonic for the last measure. Repeat this many times until you're comfortable with the key change.

4

Chapter 1

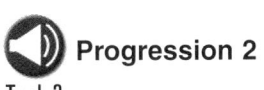**Progression 2**

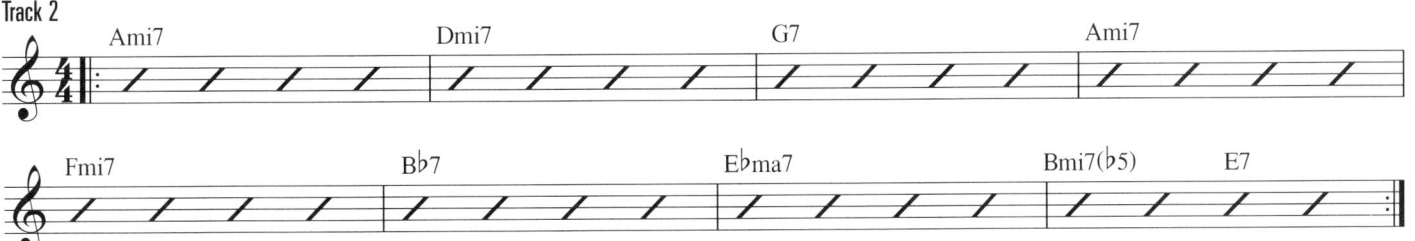

In the key of E♭ major, Fmi7 is the II chord, B♭7 is the V chord, and E♭ma7 is the I chord. In the key of A minor, Bmi7(♭5) is the II chord, and E7 is the V chord.

You have just played another key center solo. The difference between this progression and the first one is that this one *modulates* (changes keys). You can still use the key center approach, but you must change scales when the song changes keys.

The problem with key center soloing is that it doesn't clearly define the harmony (chords). Most key center solos can be compared to a pointless conversation. There is no specific or direct information being communicated. The alternative and next step is chord tone soloing.

Chord Tone Soloing

Let's look at the first progression again.

Instead of just wandering around A minor pentatonic, a chord tone solo approach would highlight the notes of each chord. For example, when the rhythm track is playing the Ami7 chord, we'll play a line incorporating the tones of an Ami7: A, C, E, and G. When the rhythm track changes to the Dmi7 chord, incorporate the tones of a Dmi7 chord: D, F, A, and C. For the G7 chord, incorporate the tones of a G7: G, B, D, and F. The musical device used to play chord tones is the *arpeggio*. Learning arpeggios and how to use them are the most important steps in learning how to play a chord tone solo.

The first step in learning to use arpeggios is to organize them on the fretboard so they are accessible and convenient. Most guitarists learn a few arpeggio fingering patterns based on sixth-string roots. If these are the only arpeggio shapes you know, playing arpeggios over this progression would require you to move great distances over the neck, from fifth position (Ami7) to tenth position (Dmi7) and down to third position (G7). This is hardly efficient and prevents playing smooth and connected lines. The next chapter deals with the organization of arpeggios so that smooth connections can be made when moving from one arpeggio to another.

Summary

- A solo that uses the scale of the key as the source of notes is a key center solo.
- A solo that uses the tones of each chord as the source of notes is a chord tone solo.
- A chord tone solo uses arpeggios to outline each chord.
- In order to be most useful, arpeggios need to be organized into a system on the neck.

What we've covered thus far:

- key center soloing
- chord tone soloing

What's next?

- arpeggio organization in major

Organizing Arpeggios in Major Scale Patterns

Objectives:

- To organize the diatonic arpeggios (I, II, III, IV, V, VI, VII) in Pattern I of the major scale to make them more accessible when changing from chord to chord. (Eventually, repeat this process in Patterns II, III, IV, and V.)

Definitions:

- **Fingering** – the exact placement of fingers on the neck.
- **Scale Pattern** – the physical arrangement of scale tones on the neck.
- **Arpeggio Pattern** – the physical arrangement of arpeggio tones on the neck.

Helpful Hint:

Arpeggios and chords are in reality the same thing. The difference is in how they are played. With an arpeggio, the notes are played one at a time. With a chord, all of the notes are played simultaneously. These two terms will often be interchanged when discussing harmony and theory in this book. At first you'll see the word "arpeggio" followed by the word "chord" in parentheses.

Organize Your Arpeggio Patterns in Major (so you can find them)

As stated in the Prerequisites section, you'll need to understand what it means to harmonize the major scale in order to proceed any further. Harmonizing the major scale (or any other scale for that matter) is the process of building a chord on each scale step. If this is an unfamiliar topic for you, a few weeks with a good teacher or a good theory book can make this mystery go away.

The scale itself is the source of notes for the arpeggios (chords) created when harmonizing the major scale. It would then stand to reason that if all the notes of a scale can be reached inside a physical pattern of the major scale, then all seven arpeggios (chords) of the harmonized major scale can be found within the same physical span of the neck. This concept is what makes the ideas in this book work. The key to this book is learning to organize arpeggios so that all seven diatonic arpeggios (chords) of the harmonized major scale are accessible in one place on the neck. Multiply this by five patterns of the major scale, and you'll have a complete picture of the neck. No matter where you are on the neck, you'll be able to find any of the diatonic arpeggios.

Following is Pattern I of the major scale with the scale degrees numbered. We'll build the appropriate arpeggio on each scale degree. The magic is that all seven arpeggios are all inside the scale pattern. Pattern I is of course, a moveable scale pattern—moveable to any key. No matter what key you move it to, the arpeggio patterns and their number designations remain the same.

Chapter 2

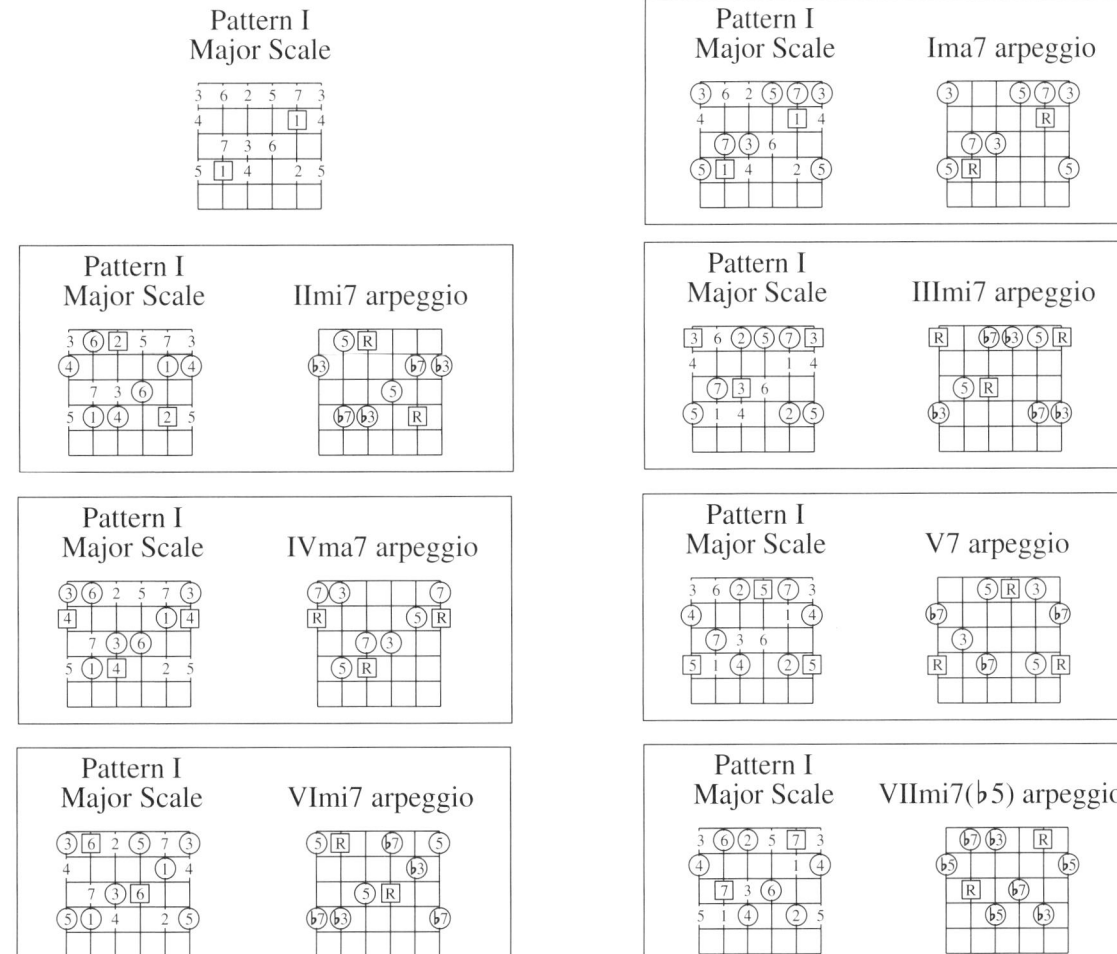

What to Practice

To get started, pick any position (and therefore any key) on the neck. Warm up by playing up and down Pattern I of the major scale. Starting with the I chord, play each arpeggio pattern from its root as high as you can go in the shape and back down as low as you can go in the shape, returning to the root. Start without a metronome and concentrate on using strict alternate picking! Alternate picking will make a huge difference in your ability to play in time and with good feel at faster tempos. Don't cheat on this! If you don't work hard on using alternate picking now, you'll pay later in the form of bad time and weak feel. Your fretting hand should remain in the same position for all the arpeggio shapes of the Pattern I major scale.

After a day or two of getting familiar with the newness of playing arpeggios and alternate picking, get your metronome out. Initially you'll want to set it at a very slow tempo; 60 beats per minute (bpm) should be a good starting point. Practice your arpeggios exactly as you did before—from the root all the way up and all the way down within each shape returning to the root using eighth notes (with alternate picking!).

Play the arpeggio patterns in succession: Ima7–IImi7–IIImi7–IVma7–V7–VImi7–VIImi7(♭5). Play eighth notes with the metronome's quarter notes. For newcomers to alternate picking, the metronome can help you play alternate picking correctly. Your pick plays a downstroke with each click and an upstroke in between each click. It's easy to mess up playing arpeggios with alternate picking at first. Watch your picking hand very closely. Get this right at the early stage of development so it won't become a big problem for you later. Over days and weeks, gradually increase the tempo but never to a point where you're missing notes or playing sloppy. Reaching new speed goals is important but not at the expense of clean execution. Play cleanly! Play cleanly! Play cleanly!

 Listen to the example on the CD, which demonstrates the arpeggios of Pattern I major in the key of F.

Track 3

Chapter Summary:
- All of the arpeggios created by harmonizing a scale (in this case, the major scale) can be found within each scale fingering pattern.
- Organizing arpeggios in this way makes the process of smoothly connecting one to another possible.
- Arpeggios should be practiced using alternate picking.

What we've covered thus far:
- key center and chord tone soloing
- arpeggio organization in major

What's next?
- arpeggio organization in minor

Organizing Arpeggios in Minor Scale Patterns

Objective:

- To organize the diatonic arpeggios (I, II, ♭III, IV, V, ♭VI, ♭VII) in Pattern II of the minor scale to make them more accessible when changing from chord to chord. (Eventually repeat this process in Patterns I, III, IV, and V.)

Why are we starting with Pattern II minor? Because it looks like Pattern I of major and uses most of the same arpeggio shapes.

Helpful Hint:

When speaking strictly about the harmonized natural minor scale, it is important to note that the *diatonic* V chord is actually minor in quality. However, in most jazz standard progressions the V chord is changed to a dominant 7 chord. This is done to bring the *leading tone* into the harmony. The major 3rd of a V7 chord is the leading tone (major 7th scale degree) of the key. When the leading tone is present in the V chord, a strong pull is felt from the V7 to the I chord. Notice the V7 occurs naturally in the harmonized major scale and gives the same strong leading tone effect.

Throughout this book, the V chords in both major and minor keys will most often be presented as dominant 7 chords as is consistent with most jazz progressions.

Organize Your Arpeggio Patterns in Minor (so you can find them)

As stated in the Prerequisites section, you'll need to understand what it means to harmonize the minor scale in order to proceed any further. Like in the major scale, the scale itself is the source of notes for the arpeggios (chords) created when harmonizing the minor scale. If all the notes of a scale can be reached inside a pattern of the minor scale, then all seven arpeggios (chords) of the harmonized minor scale can be found within the same physical span of the neck. Again, this is what makes the ideas in this book work. The key is learning to organize arpeggios so that all seven diatonic arpeggios (chords) of the harmonized major and minor scales are accessible in one place on the neck. Multiply this by five patterns of the minor scale and you will have a complete picture of the neck. No matter where you are on the neck you'll be able to find any of the diatonic arpeggios.

Following is Pattern II of the minor scale with the scale degrees numbered. We'll build the appropriate arpeggio fingering on each scale degree. The magic is that all seven arpeggios are all inside the scale pattern. Pattern II of minor is, of course, a moveable scale pattern—moveable to any key. No matter what key you move it to, the arpeggio patterns and their number designations remain the same.

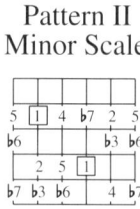

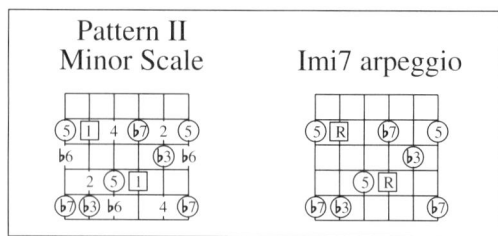

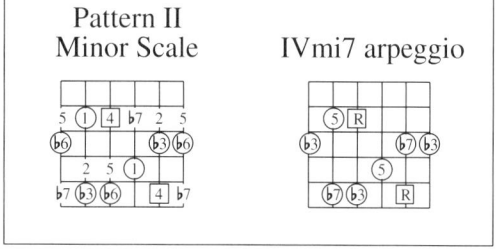

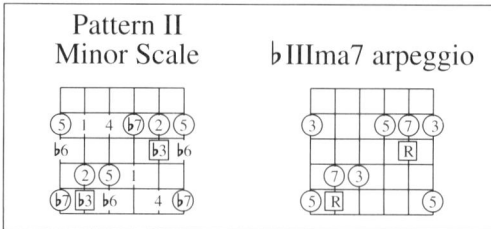

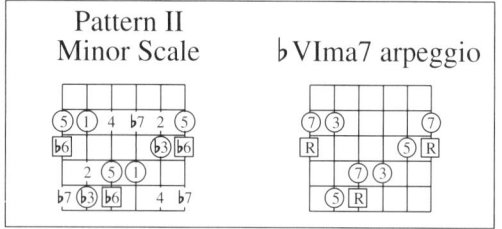

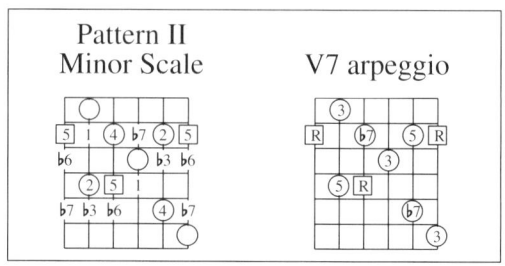

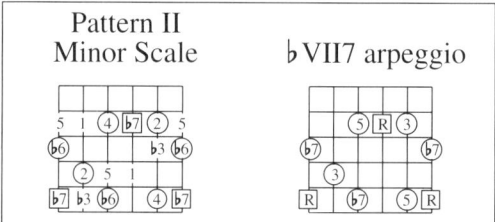

What to Practice

To get started, pick any position (and therefore any minor key) on the neck. Starting with the I chord, play each arpeggio pattern from its root as high as you can go in the shape and back down as low as you can go in the shape, returning to the root. Start without a metronome and concentrate on using strict alternate picking! Your fretting hand should remain in the same position for all the arpeggio shapes of the Pattern II minor scale except for the V7 where you'll need to shift one fret down (toward the nut) when playing the bottom two strings.

After a day or two of getting familiar with the newness of playing arpeggios and alternate picking, get your metronome out. Initially you'll want to set it at a very slow tempo; 60 bpm should be a good starting point. Practice your arpeggios exactly as you did before—from the root all the way up and all the way down within each shape returning to the root using eighth notes (with alternate picking!).

Play the arpeggio patterns in succession: Imi7–IImi7(♭5)–♭IIIma7–IVmi7–V7–♭VIma7–♭VII7. Play eighth notes with the metronome's quarter notes. Over days and weeks, gradually increase the tempo but never to a point where you're missing notes or playing sloppy. Reaching new speed goals is important but not at the expense of clean execution. Play cleanly! Play cleanly! Play cleanly!

 Listen to the example on the CD, which demonstrates the arpeggio patterns in the key of D minor.
Track 4

Chapter 3

Chapter Summary:

- All of the arpeggios created by harmonizing a scale (in this case, the minor scale) can be found within each scale fingering pattern.
- Organizing arpeggios in this way makes the process of smoothly connecting one to another possible.
- Arpeggios should be practiced using alternate picking.

What we've covered thus far:

- key center and chord tone soloing
- arpeggio organization in major
- arpeggio organization in minor

What's next?

- common situation concept

Situation Playing

Objective:

- To understand the concepts of *common situations* and *situation playing* in order to expedite the process of learning to solo over chord changes.

Definitions:

- **Lick** – a preconceived, prefabricated, and worked out musical idea created to fit a specific chord or combination of chords.
- **Common Situations** – specific combinations of two to five chords regularly found in most songs of a particular style.
- **Vocabulary** – a musician's collection of licks.
- **Common Situation Lick** – a worked out musical idea created to fit a common situation.

Helpful Hint:

The concepts presented in chapters 1–4 (arpeggio organization and situation playing) are applicable to all styles of music. Though this book deals primarily with jazz, the skills learned with this book will be usable in all styles.

Imagine a firefighter being called to put out a fire with no training or sense of what he or she was about to encounter. No doubt their job would be far more dangerous than if they had been thoroughly trained in all aspects of the situation: knowing what to do, how to do it, and how to react no matter what they encountered.

The same concept applies to learning to play over chord progressions, be they simple or complex. Examine any style of music by analyzing the chord progressions of ten or so of its standard songs. You will find that the same combinations of chords (or mini-progressions) happen again and again. Composers within a genre tend to imitate each other. Jazz standards (from here on referred to as just "standards") are no different.

As an aspiring soloist, you can use your knowledge of this repetitious tendency to your advantage. By examining dozens of standards, many jazz musicians have come to recognize the following list of common situations as essential mini-progressions to know. By extracting these common situations from standards and working on them isolated from the context of the songs, you can prepare for soloing much more efficiently. What you learn to play over one particular common situation will be applicable every time you see it throughout your playing career.

Our ultimate goal for this book is to learn to write, practice, and play licks over the common situations listed in this chapter. By learning and collecting licks (acquiring vocabulary) for these, you'll be in a position to begin the art of improvising using your newly acquired vocabulary. Listen to the example on the CD, which demonstrates the progressions. Situations 1, 2, 5, 6, 9, 10, and 11 will be played in F major, and situations 3, 4, 7, and 8 will be played in D minor.

Chapter 4

11 Common Situations
Track 5

Notice the list has many long/short pairs; i.e., the even-numbered progressions are the same as the odd-numbered, but the chords change twice as quickly.

Chapter Summary:

- Common situations are mini chord progresisons regularly found in most songs of a particular style.
- The most efficient way to learn to solo in any style of music is to identify the common situaitons and develop a vocabulary to fit.

What we've covered thus far:

- key center and chord tone soloing
- arpeggio organization in major
- arpeggio organization in minor
- common situation concept

What's next?

- the arpeggio connecting game

The Connecting Game

5

> **Objective:**
>
> - To learn the "connecting game" exercise. This important exercise teaches how to smoothly connect the arpeggios in each of the common situations. The connecting game prepares the guitarist for writing licks (developing vocabulary), which leads ultimately to learning how to solo over chord changes.

Helpful Hint:

The connecting game is hard work. Plan to spend a significant amount of time working on the material in this chapter. This is really the toughest part of the whole process when learning to play over changes. Why? This is all very new to most guitarists. The connecting game requires a different mental process than key center soloing, and using arpeggios to this physical extent is foreign to most players. It is essential, however, to moving on to the next level of soloing.

Ready for This?

This connecting game (really, the connecting exercise) will be one of the most significant things you'll ever practice as a guitarist. It is the one exercise that will train your mind, fingers, and ears to consistently play the "right" notes. For most guitarists, it's a completely different way to think about selecting and playing notes. It requires you to strictly follow these three rules:

1. Play only chord tones that belong to the chord over which you are playing.
2. Play uninterrupted eighth notes (no breaks, no other rhythms, no cheating).
3. When changing to the next chord, play the nearest chord tone of the new chord.

You'll eventually want to learn the connecting game for all of the eleven common situations, but first let's learn it over situation #1: the long major II–V–I. To prepare, memorize the II, V, and I chord arpeggios from the harmonized Pattern I major (see Chapter 2). Warm up by playing through them one at a time.

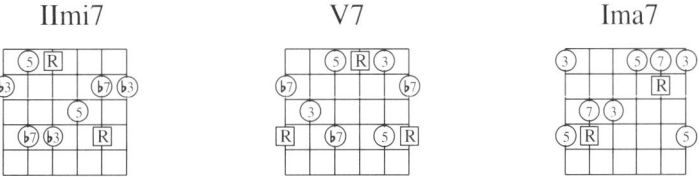

Here is situation #1 again.

To start the connecting game, be certain you have the II, V, and I chord arpeggios from pattern I major memorized. Select a note from the IImi7 arpeggio/chord (maybe the root). Begin by playing eighth notes (either ascending or descending) counting the rhythm aloud. As you play the notes of the arpeggio, count "1-and-2-and-3-and-4-and." In the beginning, counting the rhythm out will help keep you from playing too few or too many notes per measure. If you reach either the highest or lowest note of the fingering pattern before you've completed counting "1-and-2-and-3-and-4-and," change the direction of your line (ascending or descending) to complete the measure.

When you reach the last eighth note of the II chord measure (the "and" of beat 4), find the nearest chord tone of the V chord. Begin playing eighth notes (either ascending or descending), again counting aloud. If you reach either highest note or lowest note of the fingering pattern before the end of the measure, again change the direction of your line to finish.

When you reach the last eighth note of the V chord measure, find the nearest chord tone of the I chord. Repeat the process for the I chord. Remember that in situation #1, the I chord lasts for two measures so you'll need to count and play "1-and-2-and-3-and-4-and" two times.

When you reach the last eighth note of the second measure of the I chord, it's time to start again with the II chord. Find the nearest chord tone of the II chord and start over, but try not to play exactly the same notes in the same order or direction as the first time. Repeat this entire process over and over.

Note:
To avoid repeating yourself, try changing direction in the middle of the arpeggio sometimes.

Listen to the example on the CD, which demonstrates the connecting game in the key of F.
Track 6

Important!
When repeating the process, do not repeat the same exact path through the arpeggios each time. For example, if you've finished your first time through the II–V–I and you're in position to start the II chord on the root again, don't. Play a different note of the II chord nearest the final I chord note you played.

At first you'll be very slow at this. Expect to have to pause at the end of each measure to find the nearest tone of the next chord; that's normal. Memorization of the arpeggio shapes is crucial. It will take some time (a few days for some, a few weeks for others) to get good enough to play the connecting game without pausing between chords. When you feel you're ready, turn your metronome on at a very slow tempo (quarter notes at 40 to 50 bpm).

I recommend that you practice the connecting game for five minutes per situation per day. At first you'll only be playing the connecting game in situation #1 using the arpeggios from the Pattern I major scale. Eventually you will expand this to all situations in multiple patterns.

After a few days or weeks, begin learning the connecting game for situation #2. Notice that, with situation #2, the II and V chords last for only two beats, and the I chord only lasts for one measure. This is simply half the length of situation #1. Here's the progression:

Listen to the example on the CD, which demonstrates the connecting game in the key of F.
Track 7

Chapter 5

When you feel you are ready, add situation #3 (long minor II–V–I) to your connecting game practice routine. Use the harmonized pattern II minor scale. Here are the arpeggio patterns once again:

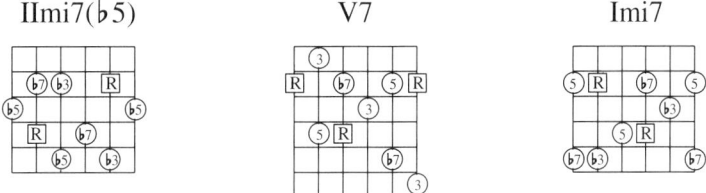

And here is situation #3 once again:

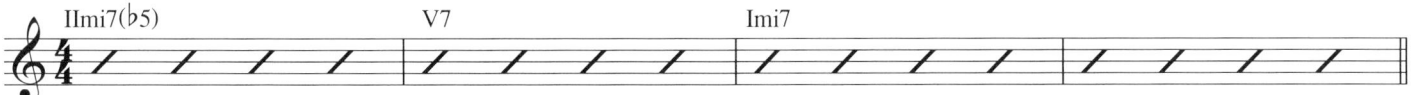

 Now listen to the example on the CD, which demonstrates the connecting game in the key of D minor.
Track 8

After a few days or weeks, begin learning the connecting game for situation #4. Notice that, with situation #4, the II and V chords last for only two beats, and the I chord only lasts for one measure. This is half the length of situation #3. Here's the progression:

 Listen to the example on the CD, which demonstrates the connecting game in the key of D minor.
Track 9

Your goal should be to become proficient at the connecting game within four to six weeks in the following situations and patterns:

- Situation #1 (long major II–V–I) in Pattern I major
- Situation #2 (short major II–V–I) in Pattern I major
- Situation #3 (long minor II–V–I) in Pattern II minor
- Situation #4 (short minor II–V–I) in Pattern II minor

Chapter Summary:

- The connecting game is an important exercise that teaches how to smoothly connect the arpeggios in each of the common situations.
- The connecting game requires you to follow these three rules:
    - Play only chord tones of the chord over which you are playing.
    - Play uninterrupted eighth notes (no breaks, no other rhythms, no cheating).
    - When changing to the next chord, play the nearest chord tone of the new chord.

What we've covered thus far:

- key center and chord tone soloing
- arpeggio organization in major
- arpeggio organization in minor
- common situation concept
- the arpeggio connecting game

What's next?

- the arpeggio connecting game in more patterns

6. The Connecting Game in More Patterns

> **Objective:**
> - To expand the number of patterns using the connecting game and establish an order for their introduction.

This chapter is a guide to expanding the number of patterns with which we can perform the connecting game. This is best done in a very specific order. The next chapter will begin to expand the note options available to us in our connecting game phase of learning.

A guitarist can be a moderately successful improviser knowing their arpeggios in just one pattern of major and one pattern of minor. However, the problems of this limitation become obvious as soon as a solo is attempted in a song that changes keys. The following example will illustrate this point.

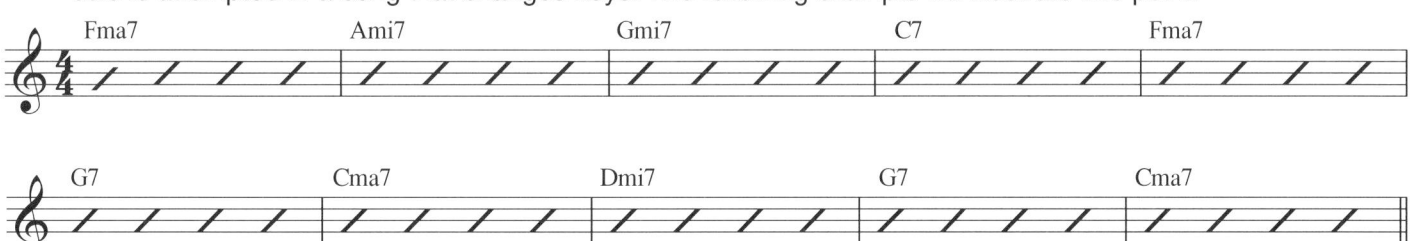

The first five measures are clearly in the key of F major. However, the next five measures are in the key of C major. Record the chords and solo over this progression with the key-center approach just using pattern I. If you only use pattern I, your hand has to move a great distance to change from the key of F to the key of C. Pattern I for the key of F is played in fifth position, while Pattern I for the key of C is played in open or twelfth position. This is physically awkward, inefficient, and the position shift makes a smooth physical transition from one key to the other impossible.

Remember—the reason for organizing the arpeggios within each key inside each pattern was to make the physical transition from one chord to another smoother. Moving smoothly and efficiently from one key to another is just as important as moving smoothly and efficiently from one chord to another. Eventually, knowing the arpeggios in all five major scale patterns and all five minor scale patterns will be important.

Now try this. Solo over the same progression using Pattern I major for the section in the key of F and pattern III for the section in the key of C. Notice that your hand doesn't need to move from fifth position to make the key change. This is clearly more efficient from a physical standpoint. Now consider how it would be to play chord tones within these patterns as well. The advantage to knowing the arpeggios in all major and minor patterns is clear. Not only are you able to move smoothly from chord to chord within a single pattern, you can also move smoothly from key to key.

> **Important!**
> I don't suggest learning to perform the connecting game in all five patterns of major and minor at this time. That's way too much to learn all at once. Instead, after you are reasonably successful playing the connecting game in situations 1 and 2 using Pattern I major, add Pattern III major.

Let's take a look at the arpeggios for Pattern III major.

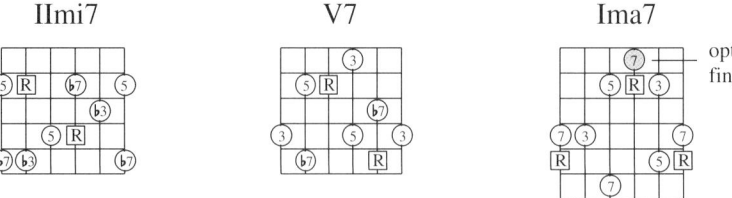

After you are reasonably successful playing the connecting game in situations 3 and 4 using pattern II minor, add Pattern IV minor. Here are the arpeggios for Pattern IV minor:

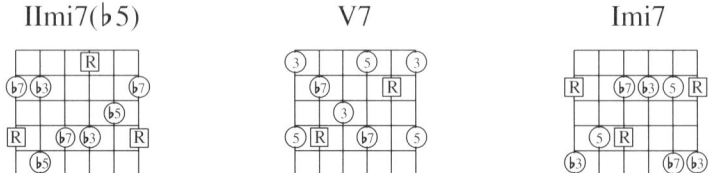

At this point, you will know the connecting game for situations 1 and 2 in patterns I and III major and situations 3 and 4 in patterns II and IV minor. This is a solid base from which you can play for a long time—maybe years.

The next step will be to start learning more colorful options in these selected patterns (Chapter 7). With the arpeggios and connecting game learned in these two major and minor patterns, a guitarist can navigate through the chord changes of most jazz standards without much trouble.

Refer to the prerequisite section of this book. Find the five major scale patterns and the five minor scale patterns. In Chapter 2 we harmonized Pattern I of the major scale building arpeggios on each scale degree. In Chapter 3 we harmonized Pattern II of the minor scale building arpeggios on each scale degree.

Chapter Summary:

- The connecting game is an important exercise that teaches how to smoothly connect the arpeggios in each of the common situations.
- To avoid logistical problems when changing keys, learn to play the connecting game in Patterns I and III major and Patterns II and IV minor. By learning the connecting game in these patterns, a pattern for any new key is only a fret or two away, creating a smooth physical transition from key to key.
- A guitarist should eventually learn to play the connecting game in all patterns in all eleven common situations, but knowing Patterns I and III major and Patterns II and IV minor well is a solid foundation.
- Practice the connecting game for five minutes per pattern for each common situation.

What we've covered thus far:

- key center and chord tone soloing
- arpeggio organization in major
- arpeggio organization in minor
- common situation concept
- the arpeggio connecting game
- the arpeggio connectin game in more patterns

What's next?

- expanding our note options

Expanding Note Options with Added Color Tones

Objectives:

- To expand our note options beyond just the chord tones to include *color tones*.
- To learn about chord families and diatonic substitution for the purpose of adding color tones.

In this chapter we will begin to expand the note options available to us when we practice our connecting game. Keeping our ultimate goal of developing interesting vocabulary (writing licks) in mind, we need to start thinking about more notes to play besides just the chord tones. Learning about chord tones and how to play them (the connecting game) is a big step in maturing as an improviser. However, it is only a step along the way. The next step is to start adding color tones.

All chords, no matter what their quality (major 7, dominant 7, minor 7(♭5), minor 7, etc.) or function (I, II, III, etc.), have additional notes besides their basic chord tones that are available to the improviser. Some can be found by simply using the extensions (9th, 11th, 13th). Others can be found by altering existing chord tones and extensions.

To simplify matters, we will follow a logical and methodical order of introduction to these color tones. In order to do this, it's a good idea to learn about *chord families* and *diatonic substitution*.

Chord Families and Diatonic Substitution

All chords in a given key can be organized into three main groups: the *tonic* family, the *subdominant* family, and the *dominant* family. Each of the three families has an emotional affect on the listener.

The tonic family, consisting of the I, III, and VI chords, evokes the emotional affect of feeling settled or at home. The tonic is, after all, the note around which a song is based. It is the key center.

The subdominant family, consisting of the II and IV chords, will make the listener feel as though they are moving away from the tonic family.

Finally, the dominant family, consisting of the V and VII chords, will make the listener feel as though they are returning home to the tonic family.

Think of I, IV, and V as being the main members of each family.

In minor keys, the organization is slightly different:

Tonic – Imi7, ♭IIIma7
Subdominant – IImi7(♭5), IVmi7, and ♭VIma7
Dominant – V7, VII°7

Think of I, IV, and V as being the main members of each family.

Notice: The VI chord is a member of the tonic family in major keys but a member of the subdominant family in minor keys.

Many progressions or parts of progressions follow a very logical path starting "at home," moving "away," then returning "home" again. Look at our situations 1–4. They all start with II (moving away), follow with V (returning home), and finish with I (at home).

Many songwriters and arrangers will reharmonize (change the chords) a progression for the sake of variation. They accomplish this by replacing the original chord with a *substitute* chord from the same family. Jazz musicians will often reharmonize songs spontaneously. For example, a progression originally written as:

Ima7–VImi7–IImi7–V7–Ima7

could be played as:

IIImi7–VImi7–IImi7–V7–Ima7

Why can you substitute the III chord for the I chord? The Ima7 and IIImi7 are both members of the tonic family. They have the same emotional affect on the listener—"home." This is called *diatonic substitution*. Try singing or playing a melody for a song you like using its original chord progression. Then, go back and reharmonize the melody with substitute chords from the same family. The basic feeling of the progression should be about the same; you've just varied it slightly.

We've just described using chord families and diatonic substitution to vary a chord progression played under a melody. But what about using this concept for melodic purposes? We can use our knowledge of diatonic substitution to introduce color tones into our connecting game, which will help our lick writing.

Let's compare the notes of the diatonic chords within each family. We'll start with major key families in the key of C.

Tonic family:

    Ima7 (Cma7) – C, E, G, B
    IIImi7 (Emi7) – E, G, B, D

    Ima7 (Cma7) – C, E, G, B
    VImi7 (Ami7) – A, C, E, G

Subdominant family:

    IImi7 (Dmi7) – D, F, A, C
    IVma7 (Fma7) – F, A, C, E

Dominant family:

    V7 (G7) – G, B, D, F
    VIImi7(♭5) (Bmi7(♭5)) – B, D, F, A

Note that there are three tones in common between members of each family.

Chapter 7

Now look at the minor key families in C minor.

Tonic family:

Imi7 (Cmi7) – C, E♭, G, B♭
♭IIIma7 (E♭ma7) – E♭, G, B♭, D

Subdominant family:

IImi7(♭5) (Dmi7(♭5)) – D, F, A♭, C
IVmi7 (Fmi7) – F, A♭, C, E♭

IVmi7 (Fmi7) – F, A♭, C, E♭
♭VIma7 (A♭ma7) – A♭, C, E♭, G

Dominant family:

V7 (G7) – G, B, D, F
VII°7 (B°7) – B, D, F, A♭

Again, there are three tones in common between members of each family.

One of the best "tricks" for adding color tones to a lick over a diatonic progression is to play a substitute arpeggio instead of the original. For example, over a Ima7 chord, play the IIImi7 arpeggio. Over a IImi7 chord, play the IVma7 arpeggio, etc.

Substitutions in Major Keys

Let's examine the substitutions for a major II–V–I chord progression (situations 1 and 2). We'll look at the substitutions for the I, II, and V chords separately. We'll work in the key of C for these examples.

Over the I chord in a major key:

Track 10

Use the IIImi7 (Emi7) chord over the I chord for a Cma9 sound.

Listen to the example on the CD. The band plays the Cma7 chord, and the soloist plays an Emi7 arpeggio (E–G–B–D), which is another member of the tonic family. The listener hears a Cma9 sound. Why? The listener hears the root of the Cma7 as the fundamental tone. The E note is heard as the 3rd of the Cma7. The G note is heard as the 5th of Cma7. The B is heard as the 7th of the Cma7, and the D is heard as the 9th of Cma7.

Track 11

Use the VImi7 (Ami7) chord over the I chord for a C6 sound.

Listen to the example on the CD. The band plays the Cma7 chord, and the soloist plays an Ami7 (A–C–E–G) arpeggio, which is another member of the tonic family. The listener hears a C6 sound. Why? The listener hears the root of the Cma7 as the fundamental tone. The A is heard as the 6th, the C is heard as the root, the E is heard as the 3rd, and the G is heard as the 5th.

23

Over the II chord in a major key:

Track 12

Use the IVma7 (Fma7) chord over the II chord for a Dmi9 sound.

Listen to the example on the CD. The band plays a Dmi7 chord, and the soloist plays an Fma7 (F–A–C–E) arpeggio, which is the other member of the subdominant family. The listener hears a Dmi9 sound. Why? The listener hears the root of the Dmi7 as the fundamental tone. The F is heard as the ♭3rd, the A is heard as the 5th, the C is heard as the ♭7th, and the E is heard as the 9th. We'll examine the V7 chords in a later chapter.

Substitutions in Minor Keys

Now let's look at the substitutions for the minor II–V–I (situations 3 and 4). We'll use the key of C minor.

Over the I chord in a minor key:

Track 13

Use the ♭IIIma7 (E♭ma7) chord over the Imi7 chord for a Cmi9 sound.

Listen to the example on the CD. The band plays a Cmi7 chord, and the soloist plays an E♭ma7 (E♭–G–B♭–D) arpeggio, which is the other member of the tonic family. The listener hears a Cmi9 sound. Why? The listener hears the root of the Cmi7 as the fundamental tone. The E♭ is heard as the ♭3rd, the G is heard as the 5th, the B♭ is heard as the ♭7th, and the D is heard as the 9th. We'll examine the IImi7(♭5) and the V7 chords in a later chapter.

Previously, we only used the exact chord tones of each chord. Now we have other options. Let's apply what has been discussed so far in this chapter to situations 1, 2, 3, and 4.

Situation #1

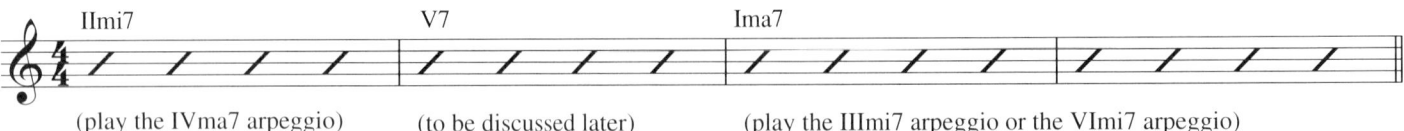

(play the IVma7 arpeggio)   (to be discussed later)   (play the IIImi7 arpeggio or the VImi7 arpeggio)

Situation #2

(same diatonic substitutions as situation #1)

Chapter 7

Situation #3

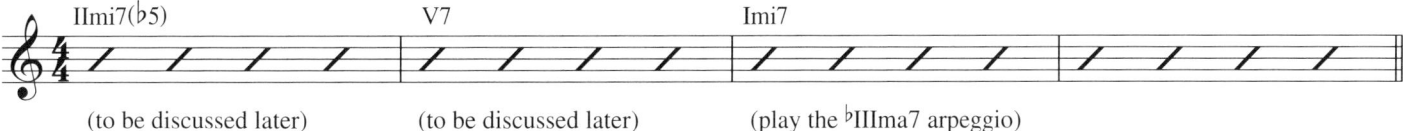

(to be discussed later)   (to be discussed later)   (play the ♭IIIma7 arpeggio)

Situation #4

(same diatonic substitutions as situation #3)

Chapter Summary:

- Diatonic chords can be divided into three families: tonic, subdominant, and dominant. Tonic chords make the listener feel at home, subdominant chords make the listener feel as though they are moving away from the tonic family, and dominant chords make the listener feel as though they are moving back toward the tonic family.
- Chords within a family can be substituted for by other chords from the same family. This concept can be applied for both harmonic (reharmonization) and melodic variation (using color tones).

What we've covered thus far:

- key center and chord tone soloing
- arpeggio organization in major
- arpeggio organization in minor
- common situation concept
- the arpeggio connecting game
- the arpeggio connectin game in more patterns
- expanding our note options with added color tones

What's next?

- the melodic minor scale

25

Introducing the Melodic Minor Scale

8

> **Objectives:**
>
> - To learn the melodic minor scale.
> - To understand the concept of using the melodic minor as a "menu scale."
> - To understand the concept of exploiting the melodic minor modes for use as color tone options in the common situations.
>
> **Definitions:**
>
> - **Jazz Minor Scale** – the melodic minor scale.
> - **Melodic Minor Scale** – a scale constructed as follows: 1–2–♭3–4–5–6–7.
> - **Chord Scale** – a scale with a very specific use over a specific chord type. Chord scales usually contain all the notes of the chord for which it is used. For example, the major scale is a chord scale for a major 7th chord because it contains all its components: the root, major 3rd, perfect 5th, and major 7th. The altered scale is a chord scale for an altered dominant because it contains all its components: the root, major 3rd, minor 7th, and altered 5ths and 9ths.

The melodic minor scale is one of the most useful tools available to a jazz improviser. One of the most convenient "coincidences" in music is how the modes of melodic minor scale are the same as some of the most useful jazz chord scales. A thorough study and understanding of the scale will dramatically change the sound of your playing. Those of you who have listened to a lot of jazz or jazz influenced music will almost immediately recognize and be comfortable with its sound. It will be "that sound" you've heard for so long. Those of you who have not listened to a lot of jazz might have to acquire the taste for the melodic minor sound. Either way, get ready to immerse yourself in the sound.

Let's begin by describing the melodic minor scale that is taught in classical theory. The strict definition of the melodic is as follows:

The classical melodic minor scale actually changes form whether ascending or descending.

Ascending: 1–2–♭3–4–5–6–7   Descending: 1–2–♭3–4–5–♭6–♭7

Notice that the ascending version resembles the major scale except for the minor 3rd. The descending version is identical to the natural minor scale.

In the jazz world, the melodic minor scale (jazz minor scale) is thought of in terms of the ascending classical theory formula only—the formula is always 1–2–♭3–4–5–6–7, regardless of melodic direction.

More importantly, the melodic minor scale is thought of more as a "menu" of notes from which to pick rather than a scale around which a piece of music can be written. Exploitation of this menu is achieved by the use of the modes of melodic minor.

Chapter 8

We guitarists are blessed because we play an instrument where we think in terms of shapes: scale shapes, chord shapes, arpeggio shapes, etc. We can actually see a physical representation of the sounds we play. We can look at a neck diagram with a pattern of dots written in and actually "see" what notes we want to play. This is a great aid when we need to memorize a chord, scale, or arpeggio. In addition, the dual-meaning of shapes that exist for guitarists streamline and shortcut the learning process. Refer back to the major scale diagrams (Patterns I through V) in the scale glossary of this book and compare the patterns to the minor scale patterns (Patterns I through V). Compare major scale Pattern I to minor scale Pattern II. The pattern of dots is identical. Minor scale Pattern II represents the sixth mode of major scale Pattern I. In reality, you don't need to relearn the "dot-pattern" for Pattern II minor; you only need to reassign where "1" is in Pattern I major. This is a huge advantage over other instruments.

Similarly, we will learn five patterns of the melodic minor scale. These five patterns and the modes of melodic minor within them will open the door to many great sounds. In this book we will mainly use three modes of melodic minor. The other modes are usable but will not be discussed here.

Melodic Minor Scale:

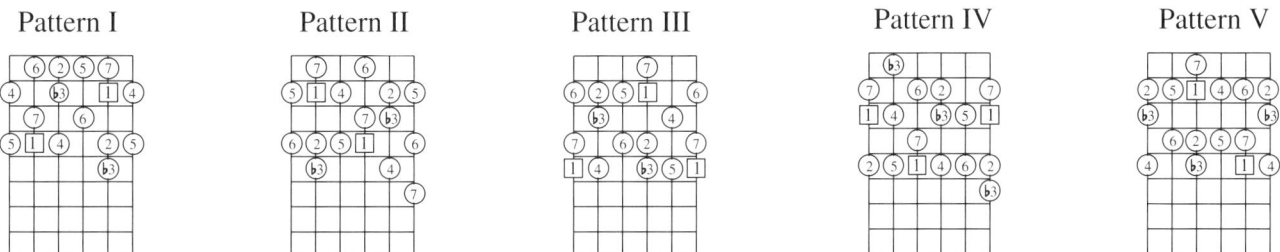

Pattern I   Pattern II   Pattern III   Pattern IV   Pattern V

For the sake of efficiency in learning, it is sometimes helpful to notice the similarities between the melodic minor scale and the major scale. The melodic minor is the same as the major scale with a lowered (or minor) 3rd. In "legitimate theory circles," this concept is not considered the appropriate description. However, it works great for guitarists. How can it help you? Think about it. Would you rather learn five completely new melodic minor shapes or take five major scale shapes (that you already know) and make one adjustment?

 Listen to the CD, which demonstrates the C melodic minor scale.
Track 14

Chapter Summary:
- The melodic minor scale is also called the jazz minor scale.
- The modes of melodic minor are useful tools to help access many jazz sounds.

What we've covered thus far:
- key center and chord tone soloing
- arpeggio organization in major
- arpeggio organization in minor
- common situation concept
- the arpeggio connecting game
- the arpeggio connecting game in more patterns
- expanding our note options with added color tones
- the melodic minor scale

What's next?
- adding altered tones

Adding Altered Tones

9

> **Objective:**
>
> - To expand our note options for dominant 7th chords.
>
> **Definitions:**
>
> - **Essential Chord Tones** – the tones of a 7th chord that are necessary to represent the essence of the chord's sound.
> - **Non-essential Chord Tones** – tones that may be left out of a chord voicing without losing the essence of the chord.
> - **Functioning Dominant 7th Chord** – a dominant 7th chord that resolves up a 4th (or down a 5th) to its major or minor I chord. For example: G7 resolving to Cma7, G#7 resolving to C#mi7, etc.
> - **Non-functioning Dominant 7th Chord** – a dominant 7th chord that does not resolve to its I chord. For example: B7 followed by Cma7, F7 followed by B♭7, etc.
> - **Extensions** – components of the chord with numbers higher than 8. The extensions are the 9th, 11th, and 13th. *
> - **Altered Notes** – chord tones changed from their natural position. 5ths, 9ths, 11ths, and 13ths are "alterable."
>
> * Note: In chord voicings, the extensions don't necessarily have to be voiced higher than the 3rd or 7th. Extensions add color to dominant 7th chords, but they don't create a stronger attraction to the I chord; they just embellish the sound.

In this chapter we will continue to expand the note options available to us in our connecting game, specifically concentrating on dominant 7th chords. We are still working toward our eventual goal of developing interesting vocabulary (writing licks). The next step is to learn to use *altered* tones on functioning dominant 7th chords.

In Chapter 7 we discussed chord families. We learned how to use diatonic substitution to expand our note options on chords from the tonic and subdominant chord families. In this chapter we'll focus on the third of those families—the dominant family. Remember that chords in the dominant family make the listener feel as though they are going home. In other words, dominant family chords pull the listener back to the I chord, which is the primary tonic family chord. The most important member of the dominant family is the V7 chord. In both major and minor keys, the V7 chord has a powerful attraction to the I chord.

Essential Chord Tones

The essential chord tones of a 7th chord are the root, the 3rd, and the 7th. Why? Let's take a look.

- root – the fundamental component of a chord. It gives the chord a name and is the note to which the other components of the chord relate.
- 3rd – defines the chord's basic quality (major or minor).
- 7th – defines the chord's quality in more detail. For example, a chord with a major 3rd and a major 7th is a major 7th chord. But a chord with a major 3rd and a minor 7th is a dominant 7th chord.

Chapter 9

Non-essential Chord Tones

The non-essential chord tones of a 7th chord are the 5th and the extensions (9th, 11th, and 13th). These notes can be absent without affecting the essence of the chord. Prove it to yourself. Play a major 7th chord and leave out the 5th. You won't miss it. It still sounds like a major 7th chord. Likewise, the 9th, 11th, and 13th are only further embellishing the chords—not defining their main quality.

Altered Chord Tones

An altered tone is one that has been changed from its normal state. For example, if you raise or lower the 5th (D) of a G7 chord in the key of C by a half step, you'll end up with either D♯ or D♭. These are altered tones. You can alter 5ths, 9ths, 11ths, or 13ths because they are non-essential chord tones.

Essential chord tones, however, can not be altered. If an essential chord tone were to be altered, the chord's basic quality would be changed. Roots, 3rds, and 7ths, therefore, are unalterable. If you change the 3rd or 7th, you've changed the quality.

Dominant 7th Chords

All dominant 7th chords can be divided into two groups: functioning and non-functioning. The definitions above state that functioning dominants resolve to their I chord, and non-functioning dominants do not. Why should you concern yourself with these two different classifications? Well, there are notes you can play on functioning dominants that would not sound good over a non-functioning dominant. The difference is important! The color tone options available to you for a functioning dominant 7th chord are very different than those available for a non-functioning dominant 7th chord. This chapter will focus on *functioning* dominants.

There are two very important features of functioning V7 chords that create the strong attraction to the I chord. I would not be exaggerating if I said the two features explained below are some of the most important things to know about harmony and the study of chord progressions.

1. **The 3rd of the V7 chord is the leading tone of the key**. The leading tone is the major 7th scale degree of a key; it usually resolves up a half step to the tonic, the root of the I chord.

Play a G7 chord followed by a C major chord. While playing the G7, focus on the B note (the 3rd). As you change from the G7 to the C, hear the B resolving up a half step to the C. **This leading-tone-to-tonic resolution is one of the most important concepts in tonal music.**

2. **The interval between the 3rd and ♭7th of a dominant 7th chord is a ♭5th, often called a *tritone***. The tritone interval is very dissonant and begs for resolution. When a dominant 7th chord resolves to I, the 3rd of the V7 chord resolves up to the root of the I chord as stated above. The other tone in the tritone, the ♭7th, resolves *down* a half step to the major 3rd of the I chord in a major key, or down a whole step to the minor 3rd of a I chord in a minor key.

These two features provide more than enough pull for the V7 to resolve to the I chord. However, just like the factory-installed engine provides adequate power to propel a car down the road, there are always those who would like to improve the engine's performance by upgrading or changing certain components. The same can be done with dominant 7th chords. We'll explore the subject of improving the V7 chord's performance in this chapter.

How can we improve the performance of the dominant 7th chord engine? We'll need to alter the non-essential chord tones. We learned earlier that as long as the three essential chord tones are present, the essence of the dominant 7th chord is clear. Including or excluding the non-essential chord tones will not affect the engine's basic performance; it simply adds to the appearance of the car. But we want better performance!

Let's take a look again at the essential and non-essential tones:

Essential: root, 3rd, 7th
Non-essential: 5th, 9th, 11th, 13th

Now, as stated above, if we want to increase the performance of our dominant 7th chord, we'll need to alter one or more of the non-essential chord tones. Let's look at all the possibilities.

Non-essential chord tones:	9	11	5	13
Altered non-essential chord tones:	♭9 or ♯9	♯11	♭5 or ♯5	♭13

Notice there is no ♭11. Why? The ♭11 is the enharmonic equivalent of the 3rd, so including it is meaningless. Also notice there is no ♯13. Why? The ♯13 is the enharmonic equivalent of the ♭7th.

Important!
Looking at the "altered non-essential chord tones" listed above, you might assume there are six. Notice, however, that the ♯11 and ♭5 are the same note (enharmonic equivalents), and ♯5 and ♭13 are the same note (enharmonic equivalents). Because of these duplications, we can say there are really four alterations available: ♭9, ♯9, ♭5, and ♯5. We omitted ♯11 and ♭13 because they are enharmonic equivalents.

The simple fact is this: Add one or more altered tones to the three essential chords of a dominant 7th chord and you have increased the engine's performance!

The Altered Scale

Let's do some addition. Three essential chord tones (root, 3rd, ♭7th) plus four alterations (♭9, ♯9, ♭5, ♯5) equals seven. That's the perfect number of notes for a scale! Since the scale we want to build contains all of the altered tones, we call it the "altered scale." To see the scale easily, understand that the ♭9 is essentially the ♭2, and the ♯9 is essentially the ♯2. Now we can arrange the essential chord tones and alterations like a scale. So the altered scale's formula can be written as such:

1–♭9–♯9–3–♭5–♯5–♭7
or
1–♭2–♯2–3–♭5–♯5–♭7

This is a piece of real magic for the aspiring jazz improviser. When soloing over a functioning dominant 7th chord, the altered scale is an excellent option as a source of notes.

Chapter 9

Important!

For the altered scale to sound good, the person comping (playing the chords) for you needs to either play alterations in their chord voicing or avoid the 5th and extensions all together. If a comping musician plays a major 9th extension, perfect 5th, or major 13th extension on a functioning dominant, they have essentially restricted the soloist from playing alterations. Sometimes if the comping musician stays "neutral" by only playing the essential chord tones in their voicing, the soloist can be free to alter 9ths and 5ths as they wish. In common practice, there are many "collisions" between altered and unaltered extensions in jazz. Tempo is a major factor in how noticeable these "collisions" are to the listener. At a fast tempo, discrepancies between the soloist's notes and the chords are less noticeable. At a slow tempo, however, greater attention needs to be paid to the interaction between the chords and the solo.

The Melodic Minor Connection

In Chapter 8, the melodic minor scale was introduced and described as a "menu scale." This means that in jazz, the modes of the melodic minor scale are more useful than the scale itself for use as chord scales over different chords. There are seven modes of the melodic minor scale. The seventh mode of melodic minor is identical to the altered scale.

Let's do a simple comparison using the G altered scale. Here are the notes of a G altered scale:

Track 15

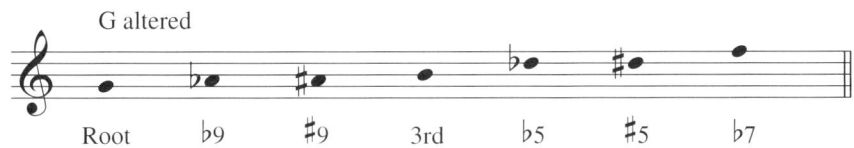

Now let's rewrite the scale using enharmonic equivalents for the sake of comparison to the melodic minor scale.

Here are the notes of an A♭ melodic minor scale.

A side-by-side comparison shows the amazing coincidence.

They're the same notes! We can say that the G altered scale is the same as playing the A♭ melodic minor scale from the 7th degree to the 7th degree. So, the altered scale can also be called the seventh mode of melodic minor. Another name for the seventh mode of melodic minor (besides the altered scale) is "super Locrian." **Put yet another way, we can say that the altered scale is the same as playing the melodic minor scale a half step up from the root of the functioning dominant 7th chord.** We will rely on this final way of explaining the altered scale/melodic minor scale relationship.

It's important for you to ask for an explanation of why we've made this scale comparison. The reason is simple. As stated in Chapter 8, several modes of the melodic minor scale are commonly used in jazz. Applying the patterns of the melodic minor scale for these different uses saves you a lot of redundant shape learning. This specific use of the seventh mode is only one example.

If you remember nothing of this scale conversion, above all remember this: Over a functioning dominant 7th chord, in order to create a stronger sense of pull to the I chord, you may play the altered scale from the root of the V7 chord. This is the same as playing the melodic minor scale a half step up from the root of the V chord.

In the next chapter, we'll learn how to include the altered scale (melodic minor scale up a half step) to our view of the arpeggios of major and minor scales. This will soon change the way we play the connecting game. We will soon be playing the connecting game using the altered scale in place of the V7 arpeggio. The next chapter will explain how we can visually organize all the information in this book into an easy-to-understand system.

Chapter Summary:

- You may use the altered scale over a functioning dominant 7th chord. A stronger pull to the I chord will be the result.
- The seventh mode of melodic minor has the same notes as the altered scale.
- The altered scale is the same as playing the melodic minor scale one half step above the root of the functioning dominant 7th chord.

What we've covered thus far:

- key center and chord tone soloing
- arpeggio organization in major
- arpeggio organization in minor
- common situation concept
- the arpeggio connecting game
- the arpeggio connecting game in more patterns
- expanding our note options with added color tones
- the melodic minor scale
- adding altered tones

What's next?

- referencing and worksheets

Referencing and Worksheets

10

> **Objective:**
>
> - To establish a concise and effective way of organizing all fretboard information learned thus far and for the future. Organization of these materials will aid greatly in the ultimate goal of acquiring vocabulary (writing licks).
>
> **Definitions:**
>
> - **Referencing** – the system of organizing all the note options (the arpeggios and scales) within the scale pattern of the tonic chord shape for one of the common situations. The benefit of referencing is the ability to find all of the related arpeggios and chord scales in one spot of the neck.
> - **Worksheet** – the page where all of the note options for a specific situation (1–11) are laid out.

This chapter is the key to making the enormous quantity of information in this book usable. Spend a considerable amount of energy on the organizational plan presented within the next few pages. Without this plan, most guitarists drown in the material.

Chapter 2 dealt with the organization of the diatonic arpeggios in the major scale patterns. Chapter 3 dealt with the organization of the diatonic arpeggios in the minor scale patterns. In both cases, we were able to arrange all seven arpeggios of a key within the four- to six-fret span of each pattern. This made the arpeggios accessible. It made performing the connecting game possible. In the long run, the ability to see all of the diatonic arpeggios within each of the major and minor patterns will make intelligent improvising possible. You didn't know it at the time, but Chapters 2 and 3 were the introduction to the system we will perfect in this chapter.

The more information you acquire about note options, the more important it will become to have a system of organizing and locating the information you've learned. In this chapter, we will use the organization system we developed in Chapters 2 and 3 to accommodate all of the new information learned since then.

In the last few chapters we've grown beyond just playing the diatonic arpeggios over the chords in II–V–I progressions—in both major and minor keys. We now know about diatonic substitution and the altered scale. We need to start organizing this information on paper in the form of diagrams. These new options will be learned and understood much more easily if we develop an efficient and coherent organizational system. This is where the worksheets come into play.

Following are the beginning worksheets for Patterns I and III major and Patterns II and IV minor. You can model all of your future worksheets after them. Notice the original arpeggio shapes are shown in the row below the scale pattern on the worksheet. You are referencing to the scale pattern at the top. Regardless of the key or neck-position to which you move the scale pattern, all of the arpeggio and scale shapes on the worksheet go with it. The ability for us as guitarists to do this is a gigantic advantage over other musicians. We have the good fortune of playing an instrument with moveable shapes. The fingerings stay the same when we slide a pattern to another key and location on the neck. Horn players and keyboard players have to deal with completely different fingerings for each key. We don't. Ha, ha!

Worksheets

Pattern I Major Scale

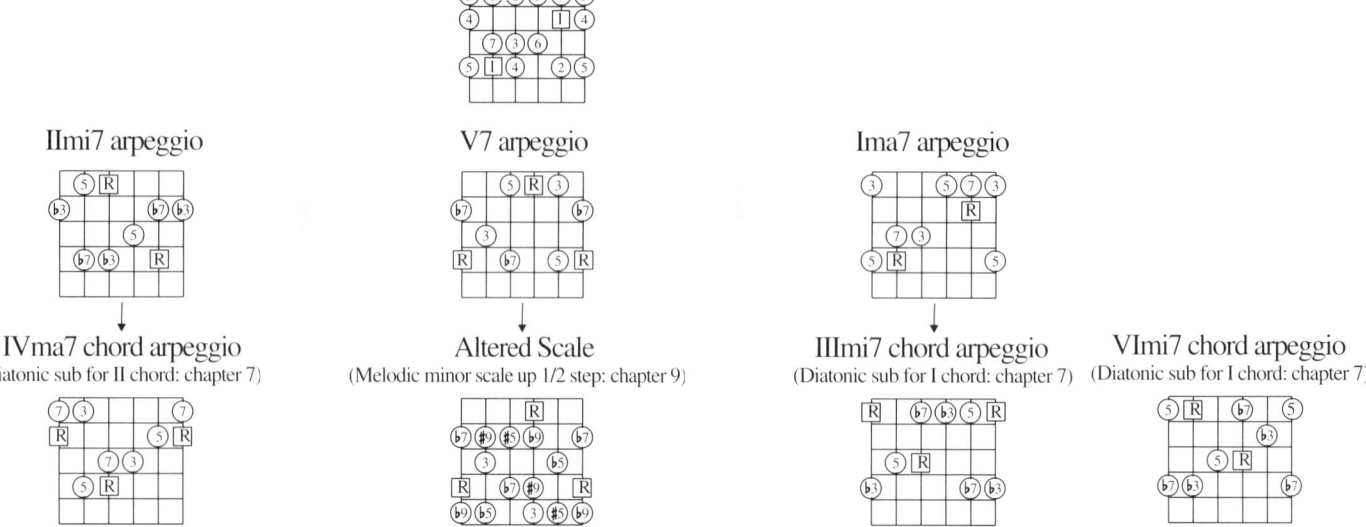

Pattern III Major Scale

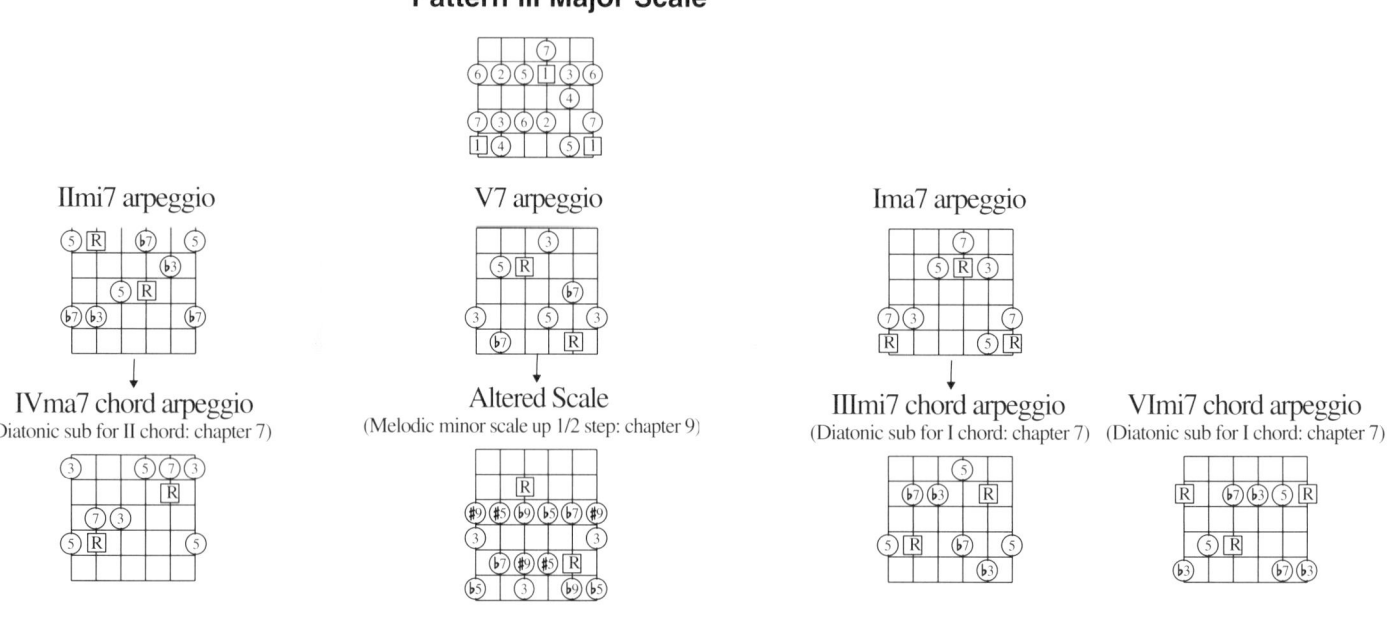

Pattern II Minor Scale

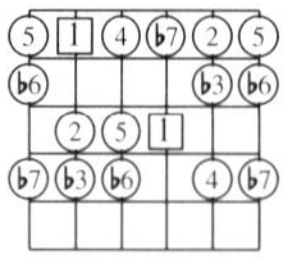

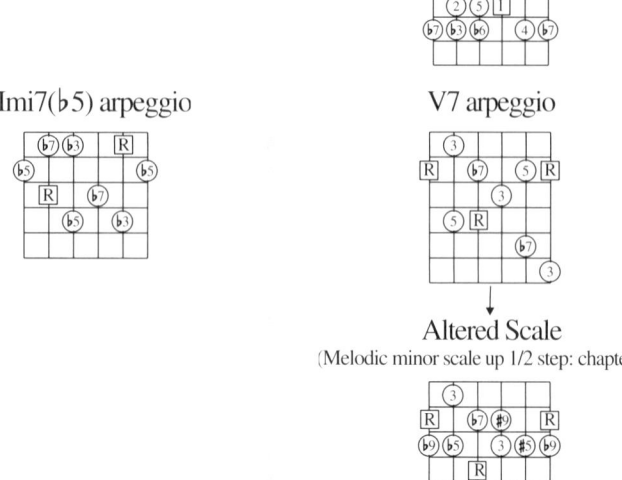
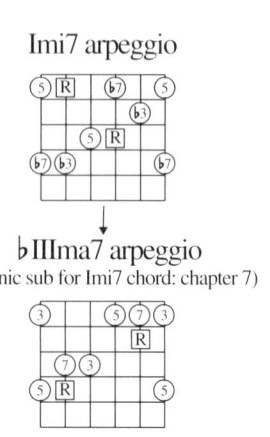

Chapter 10

Pattern IV Minor Scale

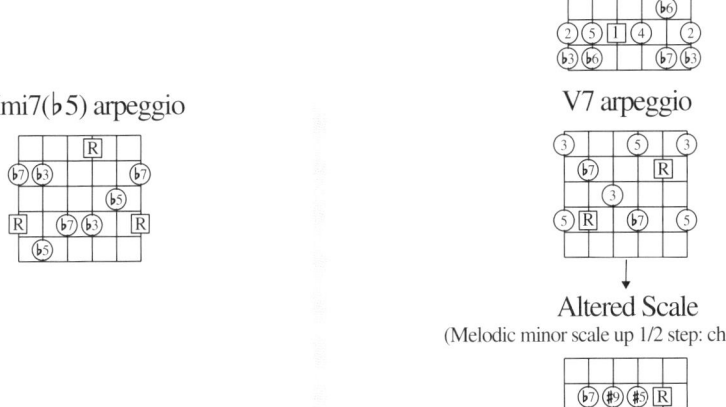

IImi7(♭5) arpeggio

V7 arpeggio

↓

Altered Scale
(Melodic minor scale up 1/2 step: chapter 9)

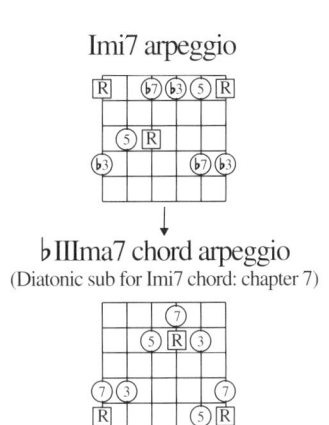

Imi7 arpeggio

↓

♭IIIma7 chord arpeggio
(Diatonic sub for Imi7 chord: chapter 7)

This worksheet idea might not look like a very important concept, but it's vital. It could be the one single concept that enables you to retain and use incredible amounts of information in the future. Remember, the ultimate goal of this book is to learn how to develop and acquire vocabulary. In order to write licks, the information (in the form of arpeggio and scale shapes) needs to be laid out in front of you in an organized and concise way.

Think of the lick as being the house you want to build. When building a house, you want to have the materials delivered and stacked in an orderly fashion at the construction site, ready to be assembled into the structure. The worksheet represents the stack of materials at the site waiting to be assembled into a lick. Eventually you'll need an individual worksheet for each major or minor scale pattern over each common situation for which you are writing a lick.

It's plain to see that all the note options (in the form of arpeggios and chord scales) are easier to see when they are laid out and organized on a worksheet.

Chapter Summary:

- The referencing concept is essential to learning, remembering, and using the numerous note options that will be presented to you in this book and for the rest of your life
- A worksheet is a piece of diagram paper dedicated to the note options for a specific home scale pattern and specific common situation.

What we've covered thus far:

- key center and chord tone soloing
- arpeggio organization in major
- arpeggio organization in minor
- common situation concept
- the arpeggio connecting game
- the arpeggio connecting game in more patterns
- expanding our note options with added color tones
- the melodic minor scale
- adding altered tones
- referencing and worksheets

What's next?

- the connecting game with the altered scale

The Connecting Game with the Altered Scale

Objective:

- To learn how to execute the connecting game using the altered scale in place of the V7 arpeggio.

Helpful Hint:

You now know that practicing the connecting game using only the diatonic arpeggios is hard work. Now we are starting to integrate some of the color tones that come with our new note options into the connecting game exercise. Your practice will now start to sound more like you are playing actual jazz lines. Plan to spend a significant amount of time on this. The material in this chapter is some of the most challenging in the whole process of learning to play over changes. The use of the altered scale in the connecting game is a big step in learning to play jazz lines. We are making the big leap from using strict diatonic notes to using all the great color tones available. Follow these rules when playing the connecting game with altered the altered scale:

1. Play only chord tones over the II chord, only notes from the altered scale over the V chord, and only chord tones over the I chord.
2. Play uninterrupted eighth notes (no breaks, no other rhythms, no cheating).
3. When changing to the next chord, play the nearest chord tone of the new chords (II and I) and the nearest scale tone of the altered scale on the V.

You'll eventually want to do the connecting game with the altered scale over all the situations with a functioning V7. Those would be situations 1, 2, 3 ,4 ,5 ,6, 7, 8, and 11. We want to ease into this connecting game because the new note choices are a radical departure from the diatonic V7 chord tones we've been working with until now. **Because the altered scale has more notes in common with the diatonic minor scale than the major scale, we'll begin in a minor context.**

Those of you who have listened to a lot of jazz will become comfortable with the altered sound quickly. Those of you who have never listened to jazz may find the sound a little strange at first. I suggest that you listen to jazz as much as possible. It's very hard to learn any style of music if you don't know how it sounds.

We'll start the process by breaking down our minor II–V–I (situations 3 and 4) to just V–I. Why? By leaving off the IImi7(♭5) chord to start, it'll be easier for you to concentrate on just getting from the altered scale to the I chord. We'll simply isolate the V–I and gradually work our way to playing a complete IImi7(♭5)–V7–Imi7.

Follow the connecting game rules from Chapter 5 when working in this chapter. To begin, follow the following four steps. Step 1 could take one day of practice for some or several weeks for others depending on how successful you've been with the "regular" connecting game.

In chapter 10, we learned to make diagram worksheets to facilitate the referencing of all the note options learned to the major or minor scale pattern. Now get your Pattern II minor worksheet from Chapter 10 in front of you. It should have the IImi7(♭5), V7, and Imi7 arpeggio diagrams at the top with the other options listed below each chord. For steps 1 and 2, you'll want to ignore the IImi7(♭5). Later we'll put the IImi7(♭5) in front of the V7 chord.

Chapter 11

Let's start. Try playing this by itself a few times before using the play-along track.

Step 1

Pick a note of the altered scale. Start playing steady eighth notes (either ascending or descending) and counting aloud, "1-and-2-and-3-and-4-and." If you reach either the highest or lowest note of the pattern before the end of the measure, change direction. When you reach the end of the V7 measure, resolve to the nearest chord tone of the I chord. Stop playing on the first beat of the I chord measure but continue counting. Listen to example on the CD, which demonstrates in the key of C minor.

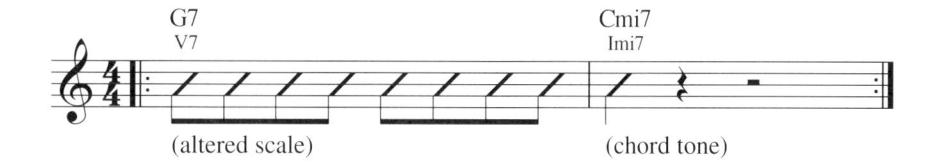

Track 16

[Musical notation: G7 (V7) — altered scale, eighth notes; Cmi7 (Imi7) — chord tone]

When reasonable success is achieved with this step of the exercise, go on to step 2. "Reasonable success" should be measured by your ability to play the uninterrupted eighth notes of the altered scale (with your metronome) and resolve into a chord tone of the Imi7 chord at a tempo of 60bpm or faster. Also, you should be able to go through the cycle three or four times without making a mistake.

Step 2

Repeat Step 1, but this time keep the steady eighth notes going through the I chord measure too. Listen to example on the CD, which demonstrates in the key of C minor.

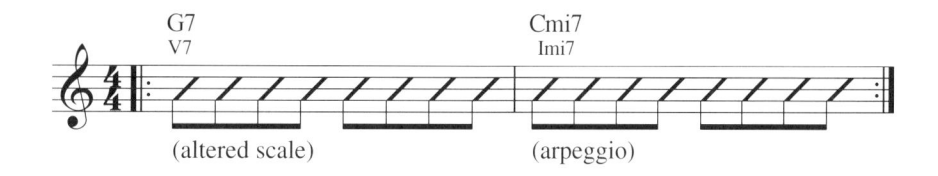

Track 17

[Musical notation: G7 (V7) — altered scale; Cmi7 (Imi7) — arpeggio]

When reasonable success is achieved with this step of the exercise, go on to step 3.

Step 3

This is the situation #3 progression. Here you'll play an arpeggio over the IImi7(♭5) chord, the altered scale over the V7 chord, and a chord tone on the downbeat of the I chord. You should still be playing continuous eighth notes up until that point. Stop playing after the first beat of the I chord but keep counting through *both* measures of the I chord. Listen to example on the CD, which demonstrates in the key of C minor.

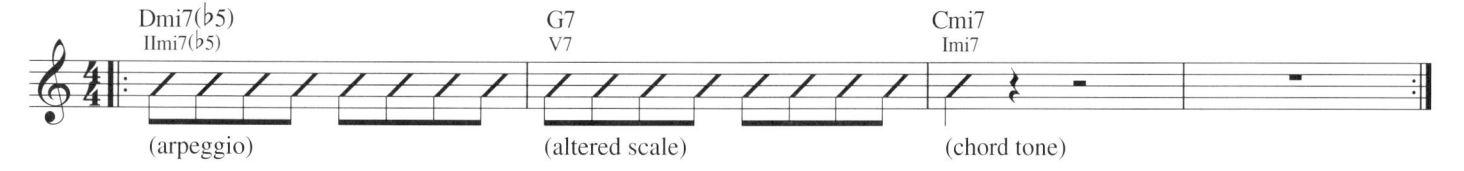

Track 18

[Musical notation: Dmi7(♭5) (IImi7(♭5)) — arpeggio; G7 (V7) — altered scale; Cmi7 (Imi7) — chord tone]

When reasonable success is achieved with this step of the exercise, go on to step 4.

37

Step 4

Repeat Step 3, but this time keep the steady eighth notes going through both measures of the I chord measure, too. Listen to example on the CD, which demonstrates in the key of C minor.

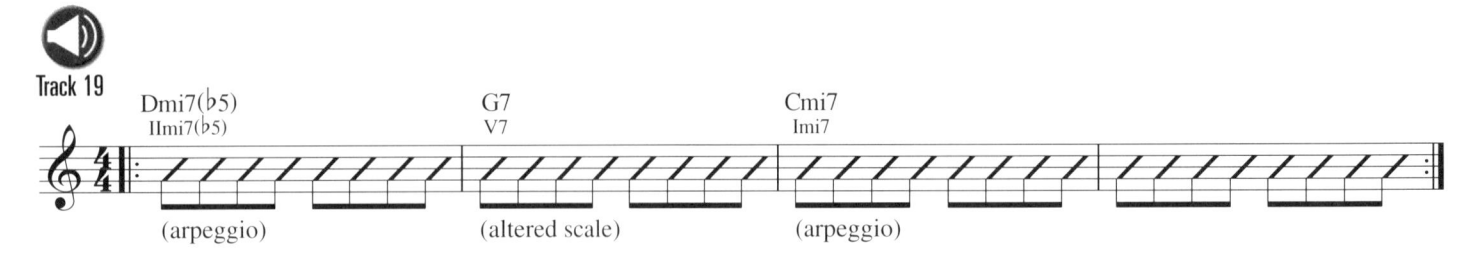

Track 19

Dmi7(♭5)	G7	Cmi7	
IImi7(♭5)	V7	Imi7	
(arpeggio)	(altered scale)	(arpeggio)	

Here are all four steps shown again, one after the other:

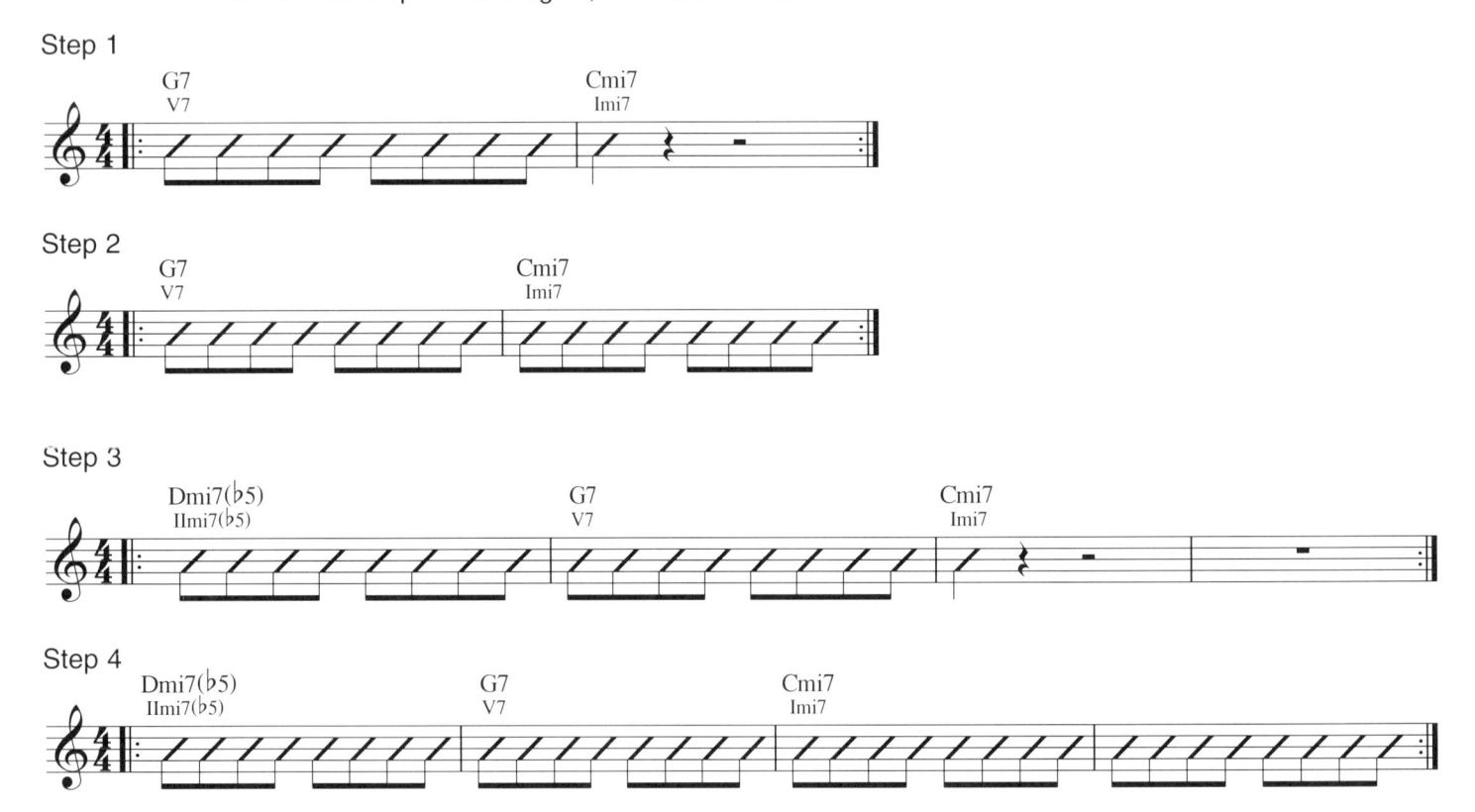

Step 1

| G7 | Cmi7 |
| V7 | Imi7 |

Step 2

| G7 | Cmi7 |
| V7 | Imi7 |

Step 3

| Dmi7(♭5) | G7 | Cmi7 | |
| IImi7(♭5) | V7 | Imi7 | |

Step 4

| Dmi7(♭5) | G7 | Cmi7 | |
| IImi7(♭5) | V7 | Imi7 | |

Now you've worked your way up to completing the connecting game in Pattern II minor with altered notes over situation #3 (long minor II–V–I). Repeat this process over and over.

Important – Again!

When performing the connecting game, do not repeat your path through the arpeggios and altered scale exactly. For example, if you've finished your first time through the II–V–I and you're in position to start the II chord on the root again, don't. This time play a different note of the II chord near the note on which you've finished the I chord.

When the time is right, add situation #4 (short minor II–V–I) with the altered scale to your connecting game practice routine. Use the harmonized Pattern II minor. You may want to do a modified version of the four-step process we used earlier in this chapter. Following is the modified version for the "short" situation.

Chapter 11

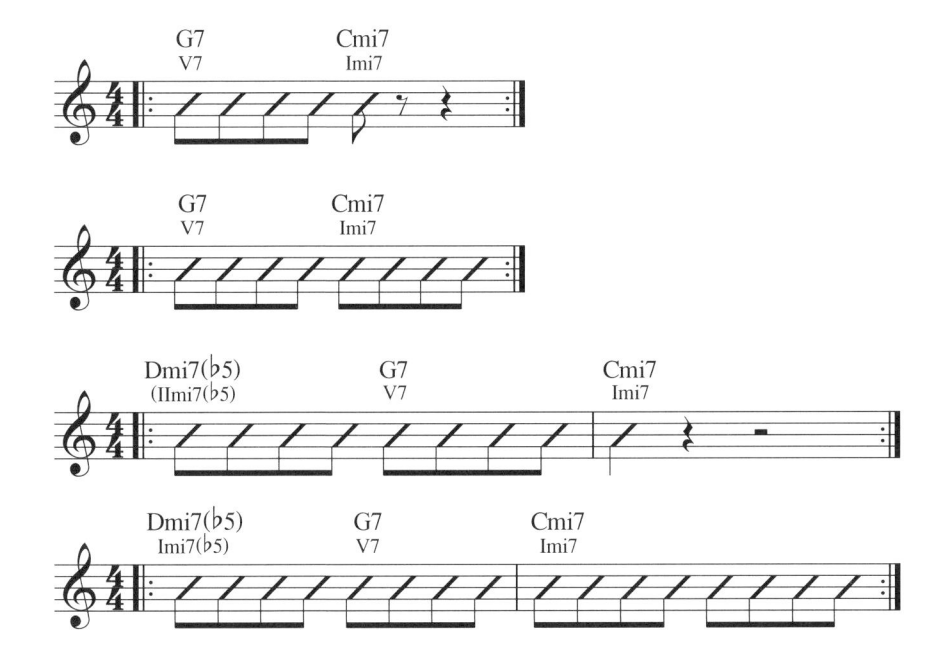

[Musical notation: Four exercise staves with chord symbols]

Staff 1: G7 (V7) | Cmi7 (Imi7)
Staff 2: G7 (V7) | Cmi7 (Imi7)
Staff 3: Dmi7(♭5) (IImi7(♭5)) | G7 (V7) | Cmi7 (Imi7)
Staff 4: Dmi7(♭5) (Imi7(♭5)) | G7 (V7) | Cmi7 (Imi7)

I recommend that you practice the connecting game with altered notes for five minutes per situation per practice session—no more, no less. You can do more than one practice session per day if you like. At first you'll only be practicing situation #3 (long minor II–V–I) in Pattern 2 minor. Wait a few days or weeks before learning the connecting game for situation #4.

When the time is right, add the altered scale to situations #1 (long major II–V–I) and #2 (short major II–V–I) for your connecting game practice routine. Go to Chapter 10 and get your Pattern I major worksheet in front of you.

Chapter Summary:
- Start practicing the connecting game with the altered scale in minor keys first. The altered scale of V7 has many notes in common with the minor scale in a minor II–V–I. Contrary to that, the altered scale of V7 has four notes that are not in common with the major scale in a major II–V–I.
- First start integrating the altered scale into the connecting game by playing only V–I and using steps 1 through 4 described above. Gradually build up to playing uninterrupted eighth notes throughout the entire situation.

What we've covered thus far:
- key center and chord tone soloing
- arpeggio organization in major
- arpeggio organization in minor
- common situation concept
- the arpeggio connecting game
- the arpeggio connecting game in more patterns
- expanding our note options with added color tones
- the melodic minor scale
- adding altered tones
- referencing and worksheets
- the connecting game with the altered scale

What's next?
- the Locrian ♯2 scale

The Locrian ♯2 Scale

Objective:

- To learn how to use the Locrian ♯2 scale as another option in addition to the mi7(♭5) arpeggio.

We've learned alternative note choice options for all of the chords except for the IImi7(♭5) found in the long and short minor II–V–I. This chapter is devoted to the minor 7(♭5) chord and what we can play over it in addition to the arpeggio.

The Locrian mode is an appropriate chord-scale match for the minor 7(♭5) chord. It's formula is 1–♭2–♭3–4–♭5–♭6–♭7. However, the half step between the 1st and 2nd degree is problematic if the ♭9 is played against the root. To solve this dissonance problem, the ♭9 (or ♭2) can be raised a half step. This alteration to the Locrian mode creates a new scale known as the Locrian ♯2 scale. In the case of the mi7(♭5) chord specifically, the ♭9 (♭2) has been changed to a major 9 (major 2nd).

Here are the notes of a D Locrian ♯2 scale:

D	E	F	G	A♭	B♭	C
Root	2 (9)	♭3	4 (11)	♭5	♭6 (♭13)	♭7

The Melodic Minor Connection

In Chapter 8, we learned that the modes of the melodic minor scale are more useful than the scale itself for use as chord scales over different chords. We learned the seventh mode of the melodic minor scale, which is also known as the altered scale or the Super Locrian. The sixth mode of melodic minor is identical to the Locrian ♯2 scale.

Let's do a simple comparison using the D Locrian ♯2 scale. Here are the notes of a D Locrian ♯2 scale.

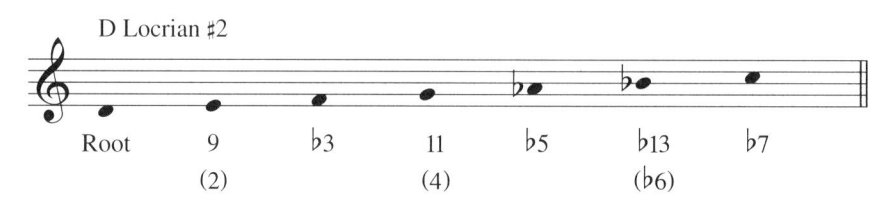

Track 20

D Locrian ♯2

Root	9	♭3	11	♭5	♭13	♭7
	(2)		(4)		(♭6)	

And here are the notes of an F melodic minor scale:

F melodic minor

A side-by-side comparison shows the amazing coincidence.

D Locrian ♯2

F melodic minor

They're the same notes! We can say that the D Locrian ♯2 scale is the same as playing the F melodic minor scale from the 6th degree to the 6th degree. This means that the Locrian ♯2 scale is the sixth

Chapter 12

mode of melodic minor. **Put yet another way, we can say that the D Locrian ♯2 scale is the same as playing the melodic minor scale up a minor 3rd from the root of the minor 7 (♭5) chord.** We will rely on this final explanation of the Locrian ♯2/melodic minor scale relationship.

Follow the following rules when doing the connecting game. First, add the Locrian ♯2 under the IImi7(♭5) on your worksheets for **minor II–V–I licks**. Be sure to choose the melodic minor (Locrian ♯2) scale that fits inside the tonic minor scale pattern.

1. Play only mi7(♭5) chord tones or Locrian ♯2 scale tones over the II chord, notes from the altered scale over the V chord, and only chord tones of Imi7 or ♭IIIma7 over the I chord.
2. Play uninterrupted eighth notes (no breaks, no other rhythms, no cheating).
3. When changing to the next chord, play the nearest chord tone or scale tone of the new chord.

Remember not to repeat the same path through the arpeggios/scales each time. You need to start with a different note each time you repeat the process.

Listen to this example of the situation #3 (long minor II–V–I) connecting game in the key of C minor. We're using Pattern II minor with Locrian ♯2 over the IImi7(♭5) chord, altered scale over the V7 chord, and the diatonic ♭IIIma7 substitution over the Imi7 chord.

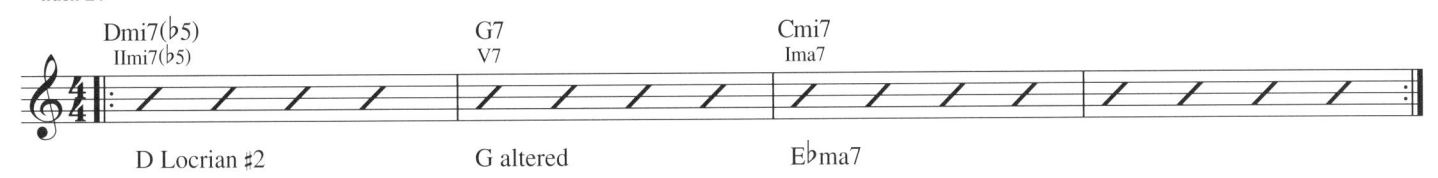

Track 21

Dmi7(♭5)	G7	Cmi7	
IImi7(♭5)	V7	Ima7	
D Locrian ♯2	G altered	E♭ma7	

Expand your worksheets for Pattern II and IV minor by adding the Locrian ♯2 scale for the IImi7♭5 chord.

Worksheets

Pattern II Minor Scale

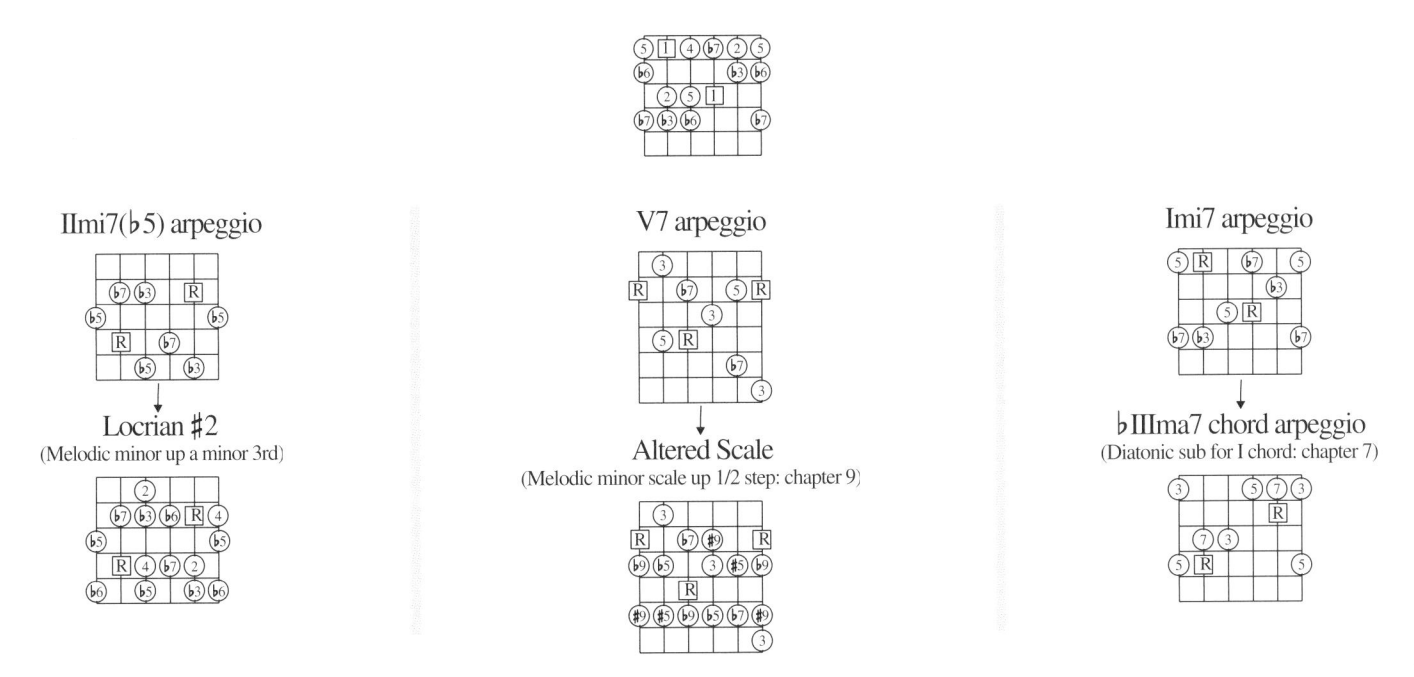

IImi7(♭5) arpeggio

↓

Locrian ♯2
(Melodic minor up a minor 3rd)

V7 arpeggio

↓

Altered Scale
(Melodic minor scale up 1/2 step: chapter 9)

Imi7 arpeggio

↓

♭IIIma7 chord arpeggio
(Diatonic sub for I chord: chapter 7)

Pattern IV Minor Scale

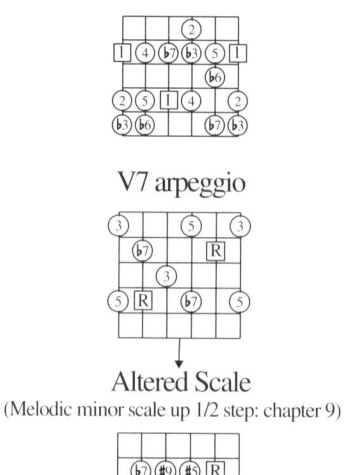

IImi7♭5 arpeggio 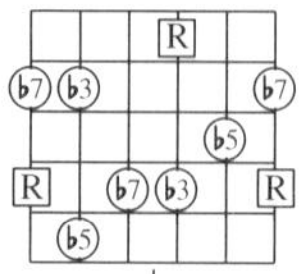 → **Locrian ♯2**
(Melodic minor up a minor 3rd)

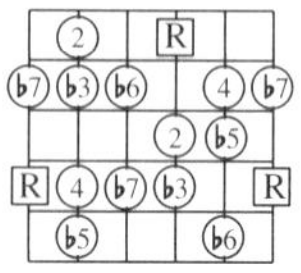

V7 arpeggio → **Altered Scale**
(Melodic minor scale up 1/2 step: chapter 9)

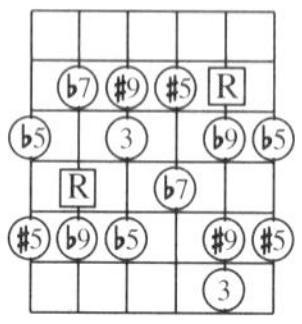

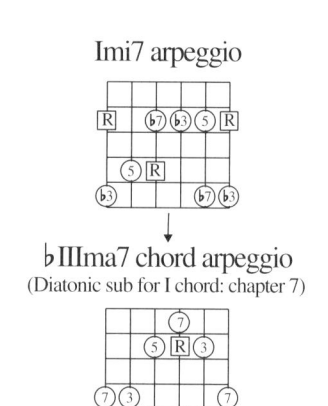

Imi7 arpeggio → **♭IIIma7 chord arpeggio**
(Diatonic sub for I chord: chapter 7)

Chapter Summary:

- The ♭9 (♭2) of the Locrian scale creates dissonance when played against the root. To eliminate this dissonance, raise the ♭9 (♭2) to a major 9th (major 2nd). This creates a new version of the Locrian scale called the Locrian ♯2 scale.
- The Locrian ♯2 scale is the sixth mode of the melodic minor scale. Another way to think of it is that the Locrian ♯2 scale is the same as playing the melodic minor up a minor 3rd from the root of the mi7(♭5) chord.
- Integrate the Locrian ♯2 scale first by adding it to the minor II–V–I worksheets and then by using it in the connecting game.

What we've covered thus far:

- key center and chord tone soloing
- arpeggio organization in major
- arpeggio organization in minor
- common situation concept
- the arpeggio connecting game
- the arpeggio connecting game in more patterns
- expanding our note options with added color tones
- the melodic minor scale
- adding altered tones
- referencing and worksheets
- the connecting game with the altered scale
- the Locrian ♯2 scale

What's next?

- writing licks

Writing Licks

13

Objective:

- To learn how to write a II–V–I lick.
- To use all of the information we've collected on our II–V–I worksheets in the construction of licks.
- To learn how to practice licks.

Definitions:

- **Lick** – a preconceived, prefabricated, and worked out musical idea created to fit a specific chord or combination of chords.
- **Common Situations** – specific combinations of two to five chords found in most songs of a particular style.
- **Vocabulary** – the collection of a soloist's licks.

The word "lick" refers to a preconceived musical phrase. Each lick is a musical phrase we write (or borrow or steal) to fit a specific musical situation. We can use it again and again. There are many similarities between verbal language and the language of music, especially when it comes to soloing. Think of all the phrases in language that we use over and over again. Phrases like "thank you" or "excuse me" are language "licks."

If you were to going to take a trip to foreign country and didn't know the language, you would probably want to learn a few key phrases to help you communicate. There would be real-life situations for which you would need these key phrases to help you get by. Think of the kind of "situations" you might be in where you would need a specific phrase to help you. These might include:

- needing to find a place to eat
- needing transportation
- needing a place to get money
- needing a place to stay

If you had to pick some specific phrases from the English language to help you with the situations listed above, what would they be? Probably things like:

"Where is a restaurant?"
"I need a taxi."
"I need to find the airport."
"Where is the bank?"
"Take me to my hotel."

You would want to know the key phrases that could help you survive until you really learned the language. Over time, you would learn more and more key phrases to expand your knowledge of the new language. Eventually, you would probably unconsciously begin combining the first part of one memorized phrase with the last part of another memorized phrase to form new phrases. These new phrases would be the product of a process known as *phrase memorization.*

What if you took the first part of the phrase, "I need to find the airport" and combined it with the last part of the phrase, "Where is a restaurant?" You would have a new phrase saying, "I need to find a restaurant."

13

Learning to improvise over chord changes is exactly like learning a new language. In Chapter 10 we discussed the eleven common situations. These common situations are the musical equivalents to the real-life situations listed previously. The objective in Chapter 10 was to find an efficient way to approach learning to solo in any style of music. By knowing the common situations of a particular style and extracting those situations from the songs for the purpose of focused attention, a musician can methodically learn how to solo in that style. Being prepared in advance with vocabulary (licks) for the common chord progressions of a given style makes improvising over the changes possible. Even if you are playing a song for the first time, improvising is possible because you have learned phrases (licks) to fit the common situations.

Remember the foreign language analogy. Even if you don't speak the language, you've prepared enough basic phrases to get by. Eventually, of course, communicating with only these rehearsed lines would feel restrictive and become frustrating. You would want to expand your knowledge of the language so that you could communicate freely. The same goes for soloing. In this chapter we will learn to write licks (common phrases) to play over the common situations. Learning licks is a great way to break into the world of soloing over changes. Our ultimate goal is to progress beyond the playing of licks to the point where we are improvising freely and comfortably. But first, we need words and sentences. Therefore, we will devote a lot of time and energy into building our vocabulary of licks.

The first licks you write should be very easy to play using simple, steady rhythms and easy fingerings. By doing this, you accomplish two things:

1. You will have licks ready to play over changes almost immediately before you grow into a more developed improviser.
2. You will have licks that will be easy to change and manipulate in a real solo.

The Moment of Truth

This is the point in this whole process where we put together all we've learned. We're going to learn to write some licks! As I stated above, write easy licks. If you make a lick too rhythmically complex, it won't be as flexible for your manipulation. Get out your worksheets from Chapter 10. You'll depend on them throughout this process.

First we'll write a lick for situation #1 (long major II–V–I). Look at your Pattern I major II–V–I worksheet. All of the options we've discussed so far for each of the three chords (II, V, and I) are at your disposal. We have assembled some very good options for note choices. Use the following rhythmic template.

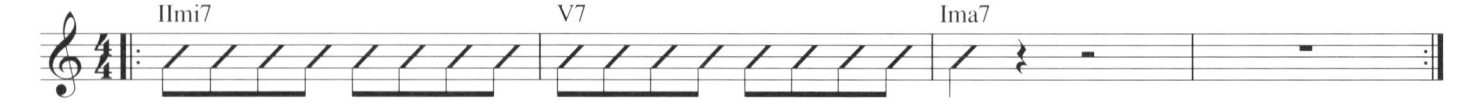

Following is a sample lick in the key of F using the above rhythmic template. Here's how I went about it:

- Over the II chord (Gmi7), I looked at my worksheet and selected the IV chord arpeggio (B♭ma7) because it's a good option as discussed in Chapter 7. This results in a Gmi9 sound.
- Over the V chord (C7), I looked at the worksheet and selected the C altered scale (D♭ melodic minor). I played an ascending line through the scale and resolved to a chord tone of the I chord (Fma7).

Chapter 13

Track 22

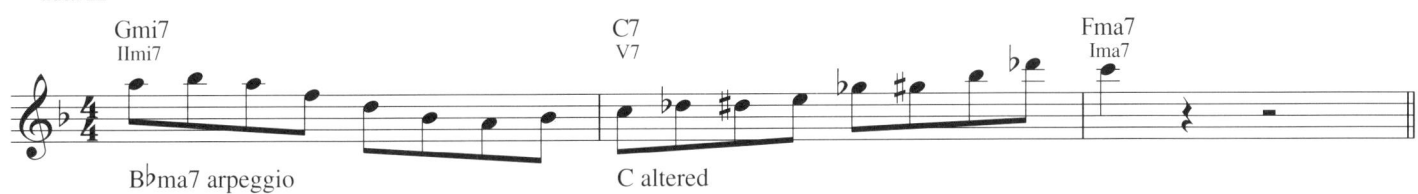

[Musical notation: Gmi7 (IImi7) - C7 (V7) - Fma7 (Ima7), with annotations "B♭ma7 arpeggio" and "C altered"]

Notice that the lick stops on beat 1 of the I chord. Why? There are a few reasons:

1. The purpose of a lick is to help you navigate your way through the chords to get to the I chord in a common situation.
2. It's easy to think of things to play on the I chord.
3. Situation #1 shows two full measures on the I chord. In real songs however, a long major II–V–I could resolve to I and then move on to other chords. If you write a lot of notes for your I chord, you might have to discard it anyway.

Here are some examples of what can happen after the resolution to the I chord:

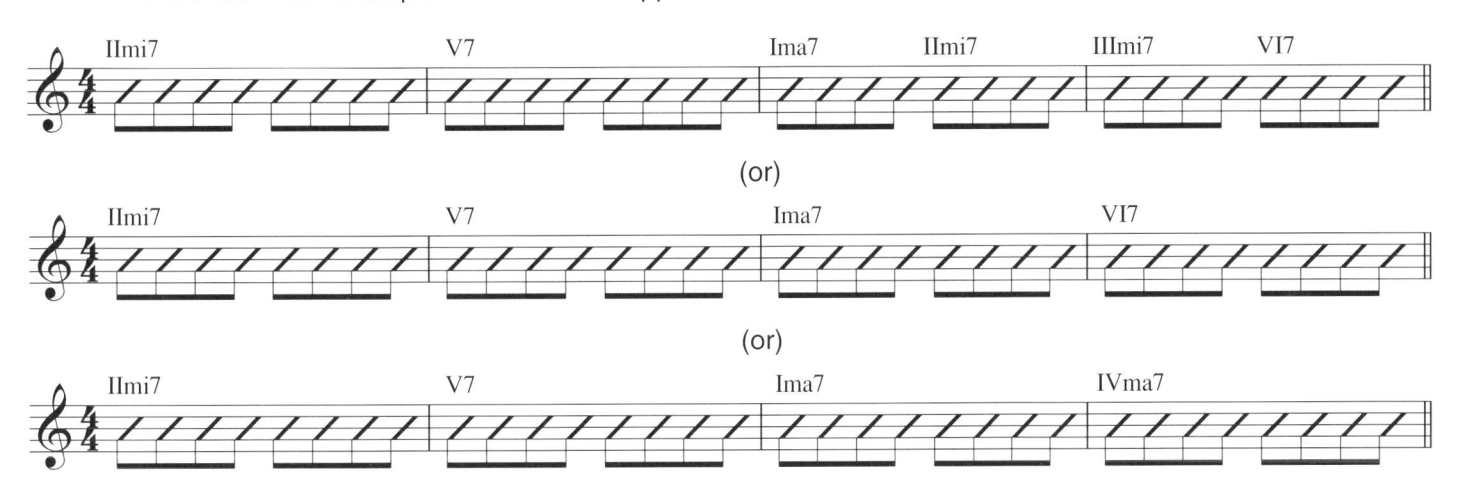

[Chord chart: IImi7 | V7 | Ima7 IImi7 | IIImi7 VI7]

(or)

[Chord chart: IImi7 | V7 | Ima7 | VI7]

(or)

[Chord chart: IImi7 | V7 | Ima7 | IVma7]

Now let's write a lick for situation #2 (short major II–V–I). Look at your Pattern I major worksheet again. Use the following rhythmic template.

[Rhythmic template: IImi7 | V7 | Ima7]

Here's a sample lick in the key of F using the above rhythmic template. I used the same exact note choices as the previous lick; I simply shortened the lines to fit the new chord progression.

Track 23

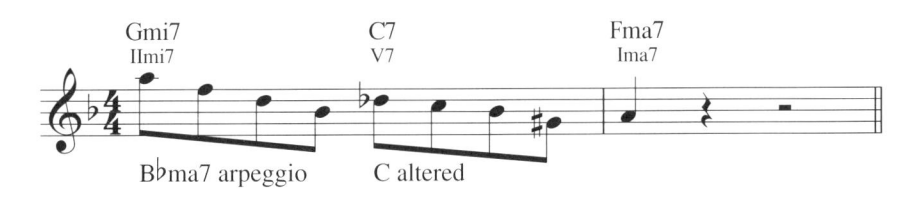

[Musical notation: Gmi7 (IImi7) - C7 (V7) - Fma7 (Ima7), with annotations "B♭ma7 arpeggio" and "C altered"]

45

Next we'll write a lick for situation #3 (long minor II–V–I). Look at your Pattern II minor worksheet. All of the options we've discussed so far for each of the three chords (II, V, and I) are at your disposal. We have assembled some very good options for note choices. Use the following rhythmic template.

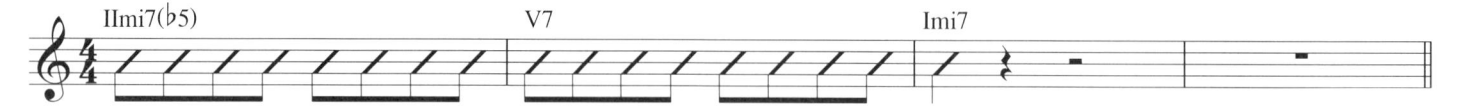

Here's a sample lick in the key of C minor using the above rhythmic template. Here's what I was thinking:

- Over the II chord (Dmi7(♭5)), I selected the D Locrian ♮2 scale (F melodic minor).
- Over the V7 chord (G7), I selected the G altered scale. After descending through the scale I resolved to a chord tone of the I chord (Cmi7). (Watch the key signature.)

Track 24

And now we'll write a lick for situation #4 (short minor II–V–I). Look at your Pattern II minor worksheet again. Use the following rhythmic template.

Here's a sample lick in the key of C minor using the above rhythmic template. I used the same exact note choices as the previous lick; I simply shortened the lines to fit the new chord progression. (Watch the key signature.)

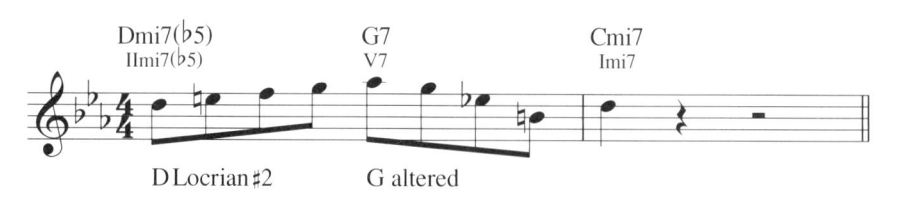

Track 25

Now it's your turn to start writing licks. You now have the tools, so use them! Organize your work like this:

- Write the eleven commons situations down on one piece of paper. Number them 1 through 11. Think of this page as your table of contents for the lick book you are going to write and to which you will constantly add.
- Organize the following pages so that each of them archives the licks you write. Chapter 1 should be your situation #1 licks, Chapter 2 should be your situation #2 licks, and so forth.
- Pick a convenient key to "store" your lick(s) in and start writing. It would also help to write a little note above each chord of each lick explaining what device you used. For example, if you used the IV chord arpeggio as a diatonic sub for the II, write a reminder note directly above the staff.

Chapter 13

To begin, I recommend writing an equal number of long and short major II–V–I licks in Patterns I and III major. I recommend writing an equal number of long and short minor II–V–I licks in Patterns II and IV minor. Developing your vocabulary specifically in these patterns will make moving from key to key efficient. Eventually you will want to develop licks in all five major scale patterns and all five minor scale patterns. However, I would stay with these first four patterns for a few years.

After you've written some licks, learn and memorize them and play them over and over. If you follow the guidelines in this book, your licks will be rhythmically simple and easy to play. You should practice your licks daily with the metronome—both with a swing feel and also with a straight eighth feel. Since your licks were conceived in a pattern but not necessarily a specific key, moving them around the neck to different keys will be easy and is crucial to your development as a soloist. Remember that the whole purpose of developing licks for the common situations is to be prepared in advance for common chord progressions. Chord progressions appears in all twelve keys, so you need to be prepared. Practice the licks in all twelve keys!

Daily practice of your licks outside the context of a song is important. This will commit the lick to memory and burn it in your muscle memory. In the next chapter, however, we will discuss how to practice your licks in context.

Chapter Summary:

- Musical licks and memorized word phrases serve the same purpose—to help us communicate when we are new to a language.
- Licks should be simple with regard to rhythm and fingering. Use your worksheets for the first four situations to write licks.
- Write your major II–V–I licks in Patterns I and III major for now.
- Write your minor II–V–I licks in Patterns II and IV minor for now.
- Archive your licks in a "lick book," devoting a chapter to each of the eleven common situations.
- Practice your licks daily with a metronome in both swing and straight eighth note feels.

What we've covered thus far:

- key center and chord tone soloing
- arpeggio organization in major
- arpeggio organization in minor
- common situation concept
- the arpeggio connecting game
- the arpeggio connecting game in more patterns
- expanding our note options with added color tones
- the melodic minor scale
- adding altered tones
- referencing and worksheets
- the connecting game with the altered scale
- the Locrian ♯2 scale
- writing licks

What's next?

- inserting licks

Inserting Licks

14

> **Objective:**
>
> - To learn how to practice licks in context.

In the previous chapter we learned the important skill of writing licks and practicing them in all keys. Every new lick you add to your vocabulary should be thoroughly learned through the process described at the end of Chapter 13.

But your licks are of no use if they can't be executed in the right place at the right time. With licks in any style, the most frustrating part of learning to use them is trying to get your hands and mind ready at the exact time when the lick is to be played. The notes you play just before the place the lick is to be inserted can distract you from executing it properly.

This chapter will present a simple but effective way to get your licks from the practice page into songs. In this chapter we'll learn to temporarily remove the distractions created by playing things other than the licks we're trying to learn. This is, of course, merely a step in the process and by no means a place to stop your development. It is, however, a step that will build your confidence in your ability to execute your licks when it's time to play them.

Let's assume that you've written two licks each for situations 1–4. We'll assume you've practiced them enough to be able to play them comfortably at a medium tempo in all keys. In order to get your licks from your practice page into songs, we'll follow these steps exactly:

1. Select a song with II–V–I progressions.
2. Plan in advance which of your licks you'll play and where.
3. Record a play-along track (or use the provided CD track).
4. Play only licks and only where the licks belong.
5. Don't play anything in between the licks.

The key to this chapter's method is to play *only* the licks. Remaining silent in between licks ensures that you can be ready to play the next lick. Start preparing to play the next lick as soon as you finish playing (inserting) the first lick. Remember, the most frustrating part of learning to use a lick in context is trying to get your hands and mind ready at the time it is to be played. By removing the distraction of playing notes in between the licks, we can concentrate on accurately executing the lick.

Now let's hear how it's done. On the first CD example, you'll hear the guitar playing licks only on the common situations. The guitar is silent in between the common situation licks. Remember that this silent time between licks is there for you to get your fingers in position for the next lick.

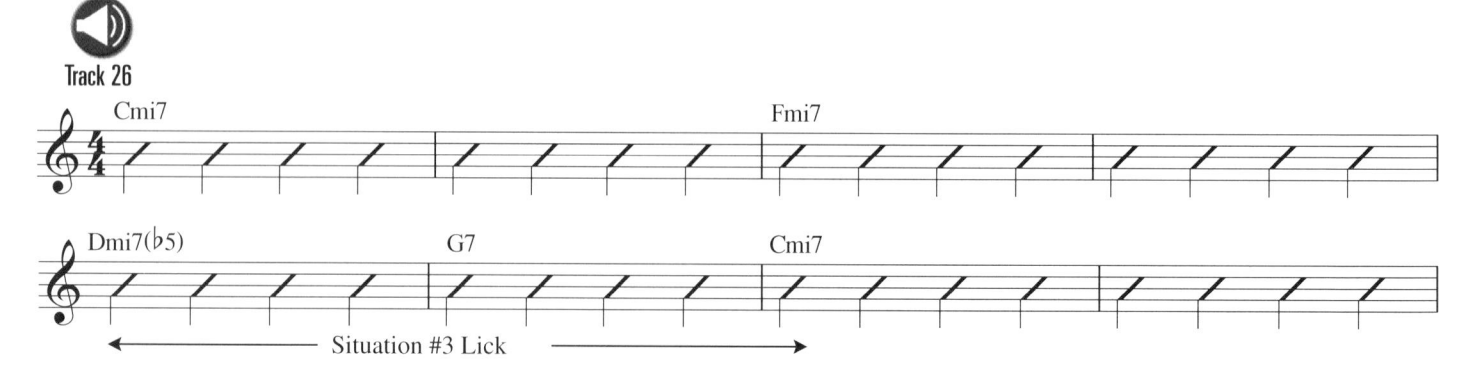

Track 26

Cmi7 | | Fmi7 | |
Dmi7(♭5) | G7 | Cmi7 | |

← Situation #3 Lick →

Chapter 14

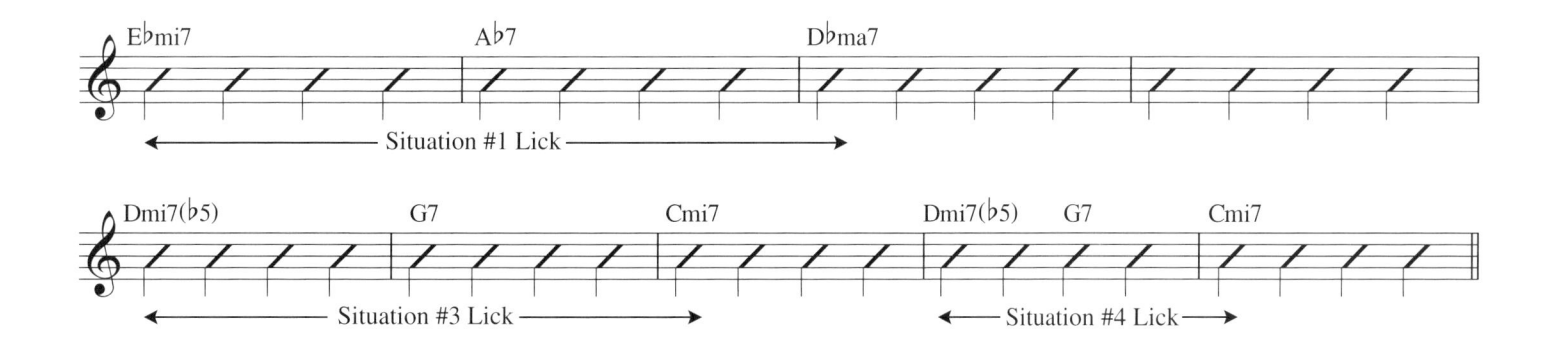

```
| Ebmi7        | Ab7          | Dbma7        |              |
|--------------|--------------|--------------|--------------|
        ←——— Situation #1 Lick ———→

| Dmi7(b5)     | G7           | Cmi7         | Dmi7(b5)  G7 | Cmi7         |
        ←——— Situation #3 Lick ———→           ←— Situation #4 Lick —→
```

Now you try. Play only your licks and only where the licks belong (see previous example). If you don't have a way to record a play-along track, use track 27, a minus-one track using the chord progression above. Here the progression is played twice through the 16-bar pattern, skipping measure 17 the first time through.

🔊 **C minor progression**

Track 27

Stay dedicated to the method; don't play anything except your licks in this stage of development. In fact, you can still use this method to work on new licks even when you've become a proficient improviser, regardless of your style or skill level.

Chapter Summary:

- The biggest problem guitarists have using their licks is remembering them when it's time to use them.
- The most effective way to begin getting your licks into songs is to practice playing only the common situation licks and nothing in between.

What we've covered thus far:

- key center and chord tone soloing
- arpeggio organization in major
- arpeggio organization in minor
- common situation concept
- the arpeggio connecting game
- the arpeggio connecting game in more patterns
- expanding our note options with added color tones
- the melodic minor scale
- adding altered tones
- referencing and worksheets
- the connecting game with the altered scale
- the Locrian ♯2 scale
- writing licks
- inserting licks

What's next?

- disguising licks

Disguising Licks

> **Objective:**
>
> - To learn how to disguise licks.

This chapter will present a way to disguise your licks so that your lines can sound more seamless. At this stage of our development, we are depending heavily on our prefabricated ideas (licks) for soloing. However, we don't want our use of licks to be obvious. Therefore, we'll first learn to put a tail on the end of our licks so their abrupt endings aren't obvious. Next, we'll learn to play notes that lead into the start of our licks so that the abrupt beginnings aren't obvious.

All the licks we've written so far (situations 1–4) end on the first beat of the I chord, the easiest chord over which to improvise. Disguising the end is easier than disguising the beginning. This is because the lick has already been played and our hand doesn't need to be in any particular position when we've finished. The beginning of a lick is more difficult to disguise because we'll need to get our hands ready in plenty of time to start the lick.

Disguising the End of a Lick

Again, remain silent in the beats or measure before the place in the music where you will play your licks. As soon as you finish playing the first lick, play a few more improvised notes over the I chord. The notes you choose can be chord tones, diatonic substitution notes (see Chapter 7), or scale tones from the key center. Pause after you improvise a few notes so you can begin preparing to play the next lick.

Here's an example of inserting licks and disguising their ending.

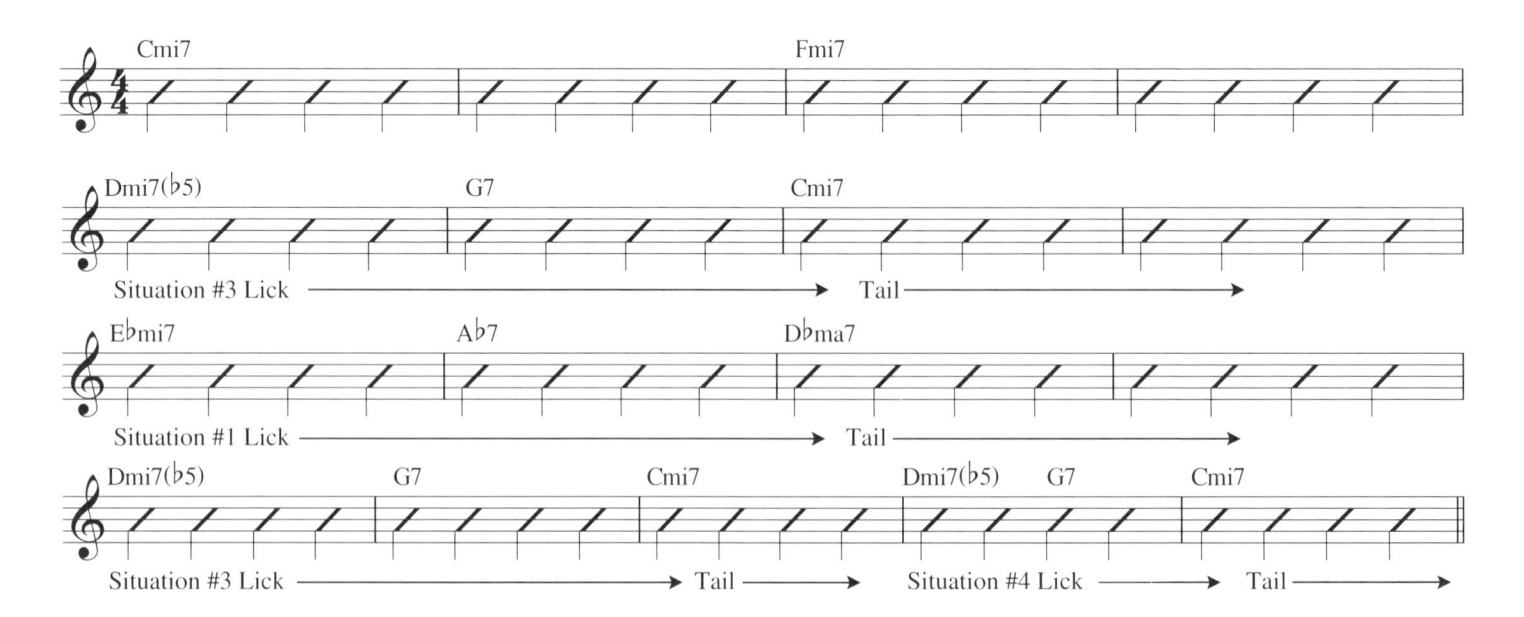

Track 28

[Musical notation: Chord chart in 4/4 time]

- Measures 1–4: Cmi7 | Cmi7 | Fmi7 | Fmi7
- Measures 5–8: Dmi7(♭5) | G7 | Cmi7 | Cmi7
  - Situation #3 Lick ————————→ Tail ————————→
- Measures 9–12: E♭mi7 | A♭7 | D♭ma7 | D♭ma7
  - Situation #1 Lick ————————→ Tail ————————→
- Measures 13–16: Dmi7(♭5) | G7 | Cmi7 | Dmi7(♭5) G7 | Cmi7
  - Situation #3 Lick ————→ Tail ——→ Situation #4 Lick ——→ Tail ——→

Stay true to the method; don't play anything but your licks and the tail during this stage of your development.

Chapter 15

Disguising the Beginning of a Lick

In order to disguise the beginning of your licks, you will not remain silent in the beats or measure before your licks. Instead, you'll play a few setup notes in advance. These could be chord tones, diatonic substitution notes (see Chapter 7), or scale tones from the key. Just make sure your hand is in position for your situation lick in plenty of time. Continue to put a tail on the lick as with the previous example.

Here's an example of inserting licks with disguised beginnings and endings.

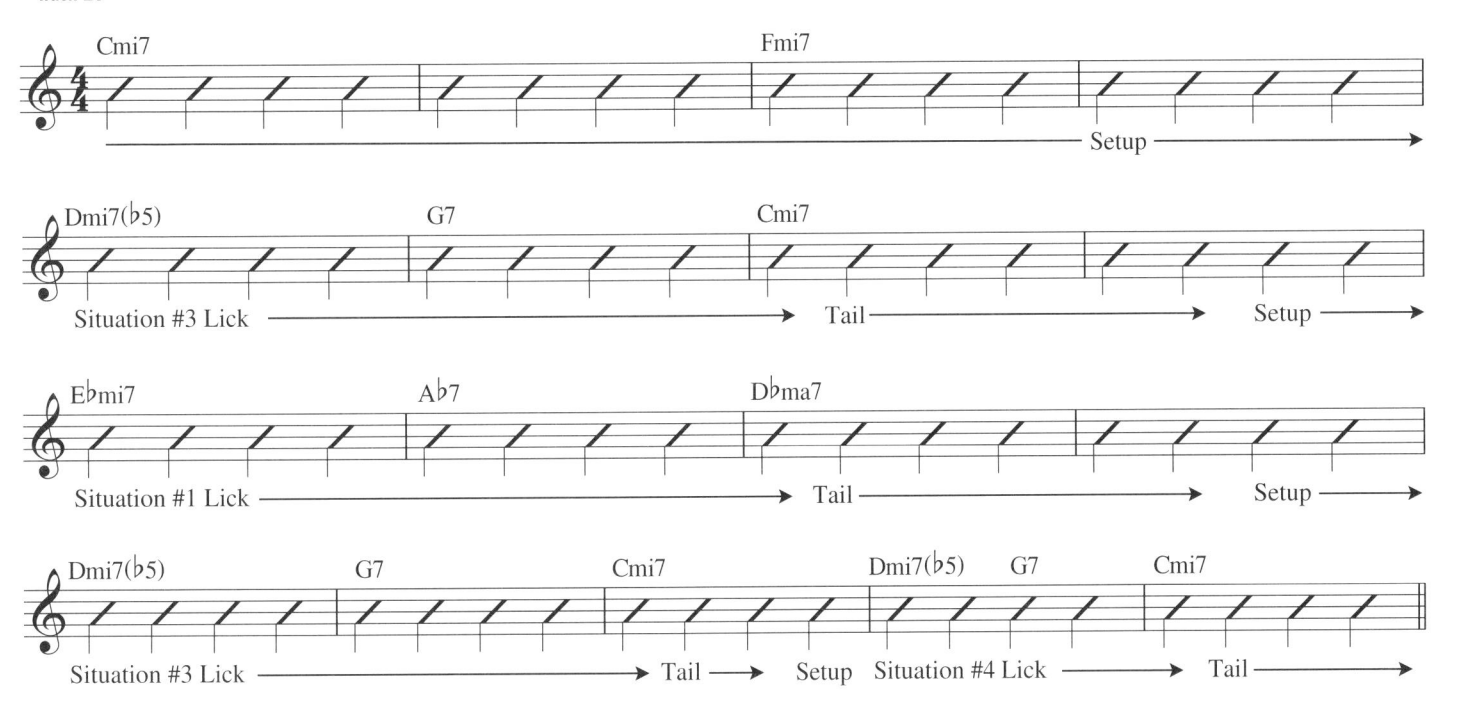

Track 29

[Musical notation showing four lines of chord progressions:]

Line 1: Cmi7 | | Fmi7 | | — Setup →

Line 2: Dmi7(♭5) | G7 | Cmi7 | | — Situation #3 Lick → Tail → Setup →

Line 3: E♭mi7 | A♭7 | D♭ma7 | | — Situation #1 Lick → Tail → Setup →

Line 4: Dmi7(♭5) | G7 | Cmi7 | Dmi7(♭5) G7 | Cmi7 | — Situation #3 Lick → Tail → Setup Situation #4 Lick → Tail →

We've reached a real milestone now. We've learned to write licks and place them in the appropriate locations within a song. We've also learned a way to "hide" or "disguise" the lick by surrounding it with other notes.

Using your worksheets, you should now make a commitment to write two licks for each of the following:

- situation #1 in pattern I major
- situation #1 in pattern III major
- situation #2 in pattern I major
- situation #2 in pattern III major
- situation #3 in pattern II minor
- situation #3 in pattern IV minor
- situation #4 in pattern II minor
- situation #4 in pattern IV minor

These licks will form the foundation from which your vocabulary can grow. Limited as you may be with only these sixteen licks, you are miles ahead of being only a key center player. By successfully writing licks, inserting and then disguising them in one song, you have learned a process that can be repeated in countless more songs.

51

Using your vocabulary you should now make a commitment to these additional goals:

- From a fake book, select a list of ten songs that are primarily made up of long and short major and minor II–V–I progressions. The list should start with songs that are simple (with only a few keys and a relatively short form). Construct the list so that each tune gets a little more challenging than the previous one—for example: "Blue Bossa," then "Tune Up," then "Autumn Leaves," etc.
- Practice integrating your vocabulary on each song using a three-step process: 1) insert lick only, 2) disguise the end of each lick, 3) disguise the beginning and the end of each lick.

Remember, your long-term goal as a jazz player is to develop repertoire and vocabulary. The above lists of goals will get you headed in that direction.

Important!

You want to "own" your repertoire. This means you are in control of the tune by being comfortable with three things. You need to know the melody, be able to solo over the changes, and be able to comp over the changes.

Chapter Summary:

- To disguise the end of a lick, play a few more (improvised) notes on the I chord after you finish your lick.
- To disguise the beginning of a lick, play a few setup notes in advance of your lick, but make sure your hand and fingers are in the right position to start the lick.
- Set a goal to write four licks for each of the first four common situations.
- Set another goal to practice these licks over ten songs that are made up of long and short major and minor II–V–I progressions.
- Your long-term goal as a jazz player is to develop your repertoire and your vocabulary.

What we've covered thus far:

- key center and chord tone soloing
- arpeggio organization in major
- arpeggio organization in minor
- common situation concept
- the arpeggio connecting game
- the arpeggio connecting game in more patterns
- expanding our note options with added color tones
- the melodic minor scale
- adding altered tones
- referencing and worksheets
- the connecting game with the altered scale
- the Locrian ♯2 scale
- writing licks
- inserting licks
- disguising licks

What's next?

- harmonizing the melodic minor scale

Harmonizing the Melodic Minor Scale for Altered Dominants

Objective:

- To expand our use of the melodic minor scale.
- To learn to use the arpeggios created by harmonizing the melodic minor scale.
- To learn the basic concept of exploiting the melodic minor scale arpeggios for use as "color note" options in the common situations.

As stated in Chapter 8, the modes of the melodic minor scale contain the same notes as some of the most useful jazz chord scales. We have already learned how to use the seventh mode of the melodic minor scale as the altered scale. This will become one of the most important tools you will use as an improviser. In this chapter we'll resume our study and understanding of the melodic minor scale in greater depth. This information will dramatically change the sound of your playing.

We have learned to use the altered scale application of the melodic minor scale as a "menu" of notes to pick from for functioning dominant 7th chords. We've incorporated the scale in both major and minor II–V–I licks. However, some guitarists who are new to the jazz sound of melodic minor have some difficulty selecting good sounding combinations of notes from this "menu" scale.

If you were to visit a restaurant and were given a menu by the waiter, you would never think to order all the items on the menu. You would select a combination of entrèes that would make an enjoyable meal. If you were to visit a restaurant that served food that was unfamiliar to you, you might order a combination plate. This would be a combination of entrèes from the menu grouped together by the restaurant owner because they go well together. Being unfamiliar with the food, the combo plate is a smart choice for you.

In this chapter, we'll apply the same "combo plate" principal to the melody menu that is the melodic minor scale. To start we'll examine this concept from the perspective of the melodic minor scale in its altered scale application. Examine the numbers below.

G Altered Scale:	1	♭9	♯9	3	♭5	♯5	♭7	
	G	A♭	A♯	B	D♭	D♯	F	
A♭ Melodic Minor Scale:		A♭	B♭	C♭	D♭	E♭	F	G

16

Remember that the G altered scale contains the same notes as A♭ melodic minor. The altered scale is the "menu." Therefore, the melodic minor scale up a half step from the root of the dominant 7th chord is the same menu. If we agree to say that every note in the altered scale is a chord tone, then it's accurate to say that any combination of notes we choose to play from the menu will be made up of chord tones. Harmonizing the melodic minor scale (arpeggios) will give us combinations of notes (combo plates) directly from the menu—note combinations we might not have thought about. The arpeggios that result from the harmonization of the melodic minor scale are very useful devices in lick building and ultimately improvisation.

Let's put this into a context. Here's a II–V–I progression in C minor:

| Dmi7(♭5) | G7 | Cmi7 |

To improvise over the G7 chord, we would probably choose the G altered scale, which is the same as A♭ melodic minor. Let's look at the arpeggios created when the A♭ melodic minor scale is harmonized and examine what each tone represents relative to the G altered chord. Remember—the notes of A♭ melodic minor are the same notes as the G altered scale.

Note:
B♭ is the enharmonic equivalent of A♯ and will be named the ♯9.
C♭ is the enharmonic equivalent of B and will be named the 3rd.
E♭ is the enharmonic equivalent of D♯ and will be named the ♯5.

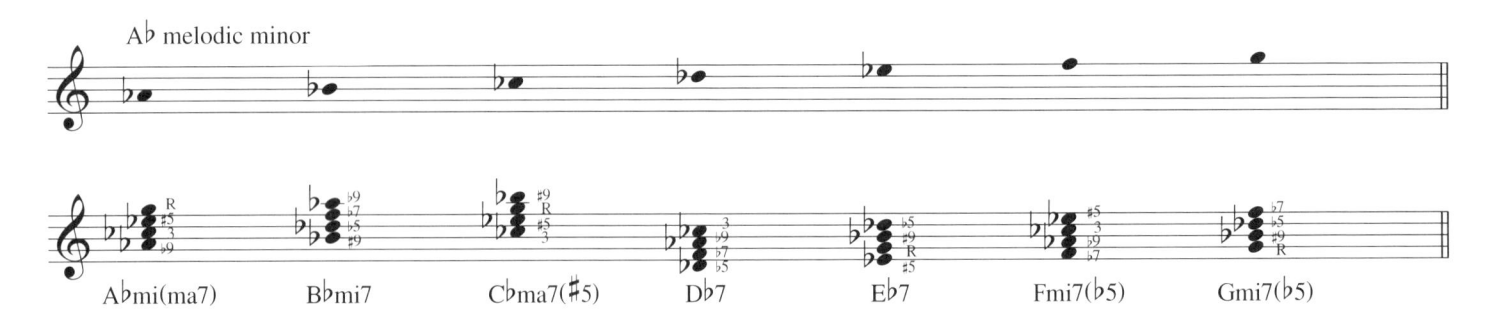

A♭ melodic minor

A♭mi(ma7)   B♭mi7   C♭ma7(♯5)   D♭7   E♭7   Fmi7(♭5)   Gmi7(♭5)

All seven of these arpeggios are viable note combinations (combo plates) of the altered scale menu. Most of us would never dream of playing an A♭mi(ma7) arpeggio or C♭ma7 arpeggio over a G7. Those ideas just wouldn't come to mind. We're introduced to these ideas only because we learned about harmonizing the melodic minor scale.

Looking at all seven arpeggios listed above could make your head spin. Keep this information in perspective. It's ridiculous to try to integrate all seven into every single melodic minor application at this time. However, working one or two into each of your licks is reasonable and worthwhile.

I suggest starting with the first and third arpeggios: the mi(ma7) and the ma7(♯5). Let's add these two arpeggios to our worksheets as choices for the V7 chord.

Note:
When adding any new scale or arpeggio choice to your worksheets, be sure they fit within the four- or five-fret span of the scale pattern for the I chord. Remember—this is the concept we call "referencing."

Chapter 16

Worksheets

Pattern I Major

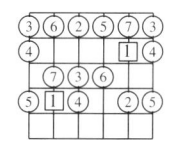

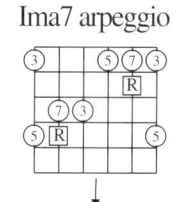

IImi7 arpeggio

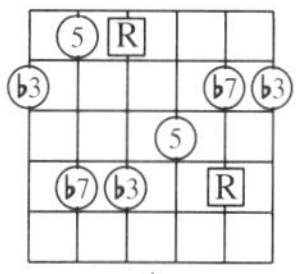

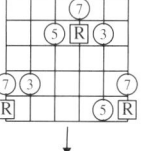

V7 arpeggio

Ima7 arpeggio

↓

↓

IVma7 chord arpeggio
(Diatonic sub for II chord: chapter 7)

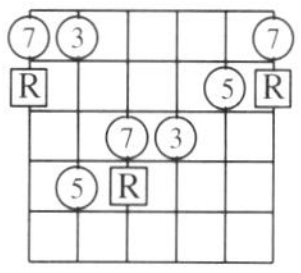

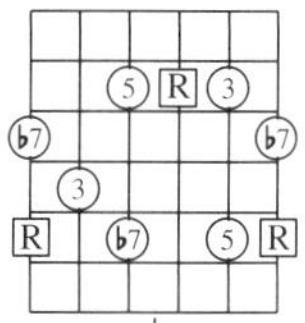

Altered Scale
(Melodic minor scale up 1/2 step: chapter 9)

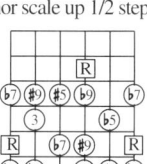

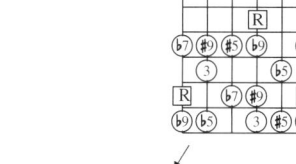

IIImi7 chord arpeggio
(Diatonic sub for I chord: chapter 7)

↙   ↘

Mi(ma7) arpeggio
(I chord from melodic minor)

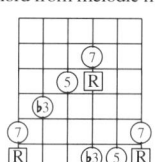

Ma7(♯5) arpeggio
(III chord from melodic minor)

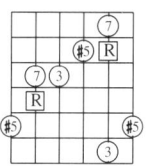

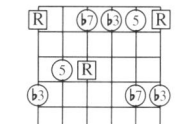

Pattern III Major

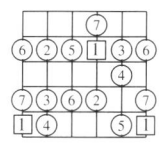

IImi7 arpeggio

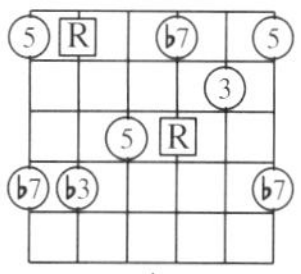

V7 arpeggio

Ima7 arpeggio

↓

↓

IVma7 chord arpeggio
(Diatonic sub for II chord: chapter 7)

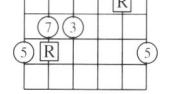

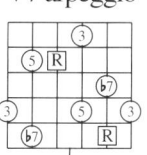

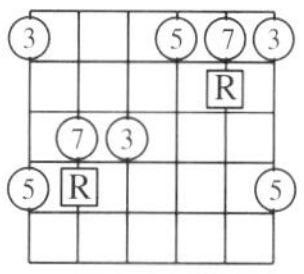

Altered Scale
(Melodic minor scale up 1/2 step: chapter 9)

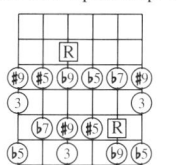

IIImi7 chord arpeggio
(Diatonic sub for I chord: chapter 7)

↙   ↘

Mi(ma7) arpeggio
(I chord from melodic minor)

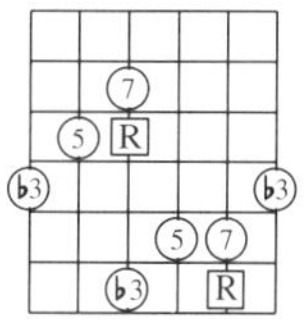

Ma7(♯5) arpeggio
(III chord from melodic minor)

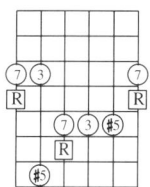

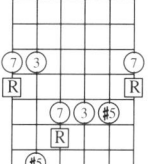

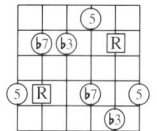

16

Pattern II Minor

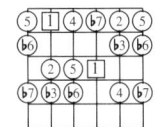

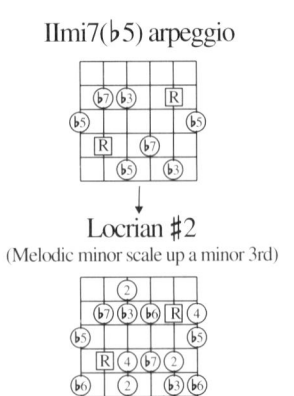

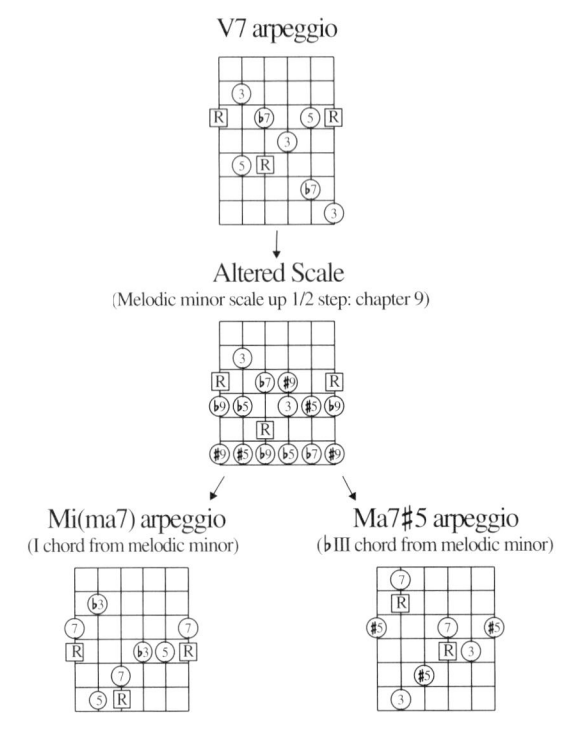

IImi7(♭5) arpeggio

↓

Locrian #2
(Melodic minor scale up a minor 3rd)

V7 arpeggio

↓

Altered Scale
(Melodic minor scale up 1/2 step: chapter 9)

Mi(ma7) arpeggio
(I chord from melodic minor)

Ma7#5 arpeggio
(♭III chord from melodic minor)

Imi7 arpeggio

↓

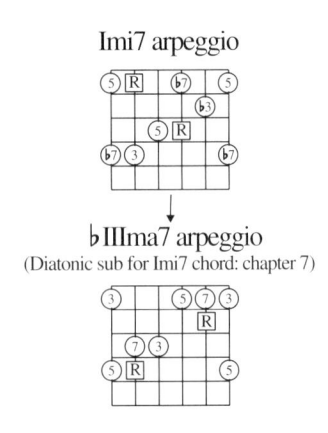

♭IIIma7 arpeggio
(Diatonic sub for Imi7 chord: chapter 7)

Pattern IV Minor

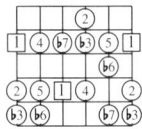

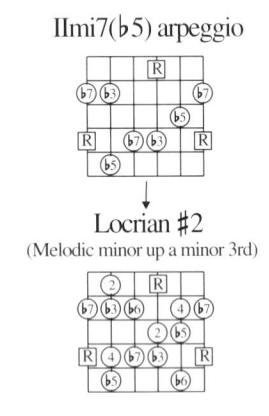

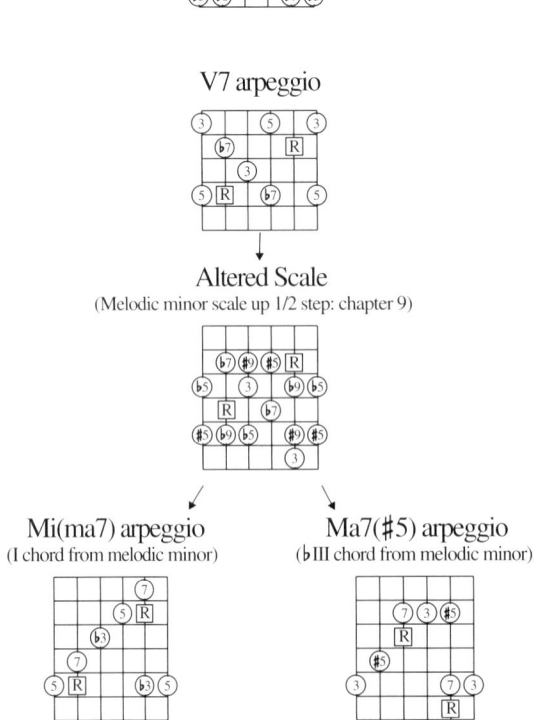

IImi7(♭5) arpeggio

↓

Locrian #2
(Melodic minor up a minor 3rd)

V7 arpeggio

↓

Altered Scale
(Melodic minor scale up 1/2 step: chapter 9)

Mi(ma7) arpeggio
(I chord from melodic minor)

Ma7(#5) arpeggio
(♭III chord from melodic minor)

Imi7 arpeggio

↓

♭IIIma7 chord arpeggio
(Diatonic sub for Imi7 chord: chapter 7)

Chapter 16

Let's hear what this type of idea sounds like. Here's a sample lick in the key of C minor using Pattern II. The lick uses D Locrian ♯2 (F melodic minor) over the IImi7(♭5) chord, an A♭mi(ma7) arpeggio over the V7 chord, and resolves to the 9th of the the I chord. (Watch the key signature.)

Track 30

Chapter Summary:

- All of the notes of the altered scale are chord tones of an altered dominant 7th chord (essential chord tones and altered extensions). The notes of the altered scale are the same as the notes of the melodic minor scale up a half step. Therefore, all the notes of this melodic minor scale are chord tones of the altered dominant 7th chord.
- Harmonizing the melodic minor scale (arpeggios) will give us combinations of notes we'll call "combo plates." Focus on using the first and third arpeggios from the harmonized melodic minor scale.
- Add these new arpeggio choices to your worksheets. Be sure they fit within the four- or five-fret span of the scale pattern for the I chord.

What we've covered thus far:

- key center and chord tone soloing
- arpeggio organization in major
- arpeggio organization in minor
- common situation concept
- the arpeggio connecting game
- the arpeggio connecting game in more patterns
- expanding our note options with added color tones
- the melodic minor scale
- adding altered tones
- referencing and worksheets
- the connecting game with the altered scale
- the Locrian ♯2 scale
- writing licks
- inserting licks
- disguising licks
- harmonizing the melodic minor scale for altered dominants

What's next?

- harmonizing the melodic minor scale for minor 7(♭5) chords

17. Harmonizing the Melodic Minor Scale for Minor 7(♭5) Chords

> **Objective:**
> - To expand our use of the melodic minor scale.
> - To learn to use the arpeggios created by harmonizing the melodic minor scale for mi7(♭5) chords.

In Chapter 16 we harmonized the melodic minor scale for the purpose of forming good combinations of tones from the altered scale. We learned to use these combinations as a source of ideas over dominant chords. In Chapter 12 we learned about the Locrian ♯2 scale and how it can be used over a mi7(♭5) chord. We learned the connection between Locrian ♯2 and the melodic minor up a minor 3rd from the root of the mi7(♭5) chord.

In this chapter we'll apply the same "combo plate" principal to the melody-menu that is the Locrian ♯2 application of the melodic minor scale. Examine the numbers below.

D Locrian ♯2 Scale:	1	2 (9)	♭3	4 (11)	♭5	♭6 (♭13)	♭7		
	D	E	F	G	A♭	B♭	C		
F Melodic Minor Scale:			F	G	A♭	B♭	C	D	E

Remember that the D Locrian ♯2 scale contains the same notes as the F melodic minor scale. The Locrian ♯2 scale is the "menu." Therefore, the melodic minor scale up a minor 3rd from the root of the mi7(♭5) chord is the same menu. If we agree to say that every note in the Locrian ♯2 scale is a chord tone or extension, then it's safe to say that any combination of notes we choose to play from the menu will be made up of chord tones. Harmonizing the melodic minor scale (arpeggios) will give us combinations of notes we might not have thought about.

Let's put this into a context. Here's a II–V–I progression in C minor:

Dmi7(♭5) | G7 | Cmi7 | / / / /

Over the Dmi7(♭5) chord we would probably choose the D Locrian ♯2 scale, which is the same as F melodic minor. Let's look at the arpeggios created when the F melodic minor scale is harmonized and examine what each tone represents relative to the Dmi7(♭5) chord.

Chapter 17

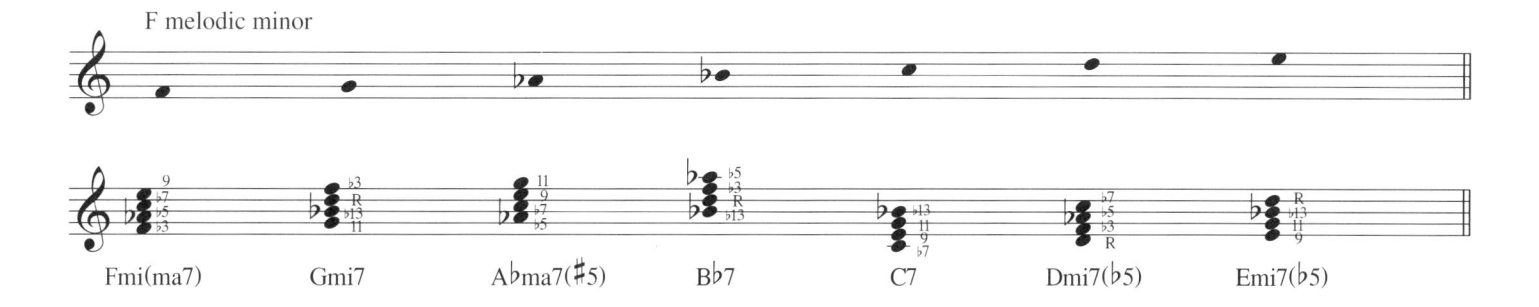

[F melodic minor scale and diatonic seventh chord arpeggios: Fmi(ma7), Gmi7, A♭ma7(♯5), B♭7, C7, Dmi7(♭5), Emi7(♭5)]

Looking at all seven arpeggios listed above could make your head spin. Keep this information in perspective. It's ridiculous to try to integrate all seven into every single melodic minor application at this time. However, working one or two into each of your licks is reasonable and worthwhile.

I suggest starting with the first and third arpeggios: the mi(ma7) and the ma7(♯5). Let's add these two arpeggios to our worksheets as choices for the mi7(♭5) chord.

Note:

When adding any new scale or arpeggio choice to your worksheets, be sure they fit within the four- or five-fret span of the scale pattern for the I chord. Remember—this is the concept we call "referencing."

This application will only be used in minor II–V–I progressions where mi7(♭5) chords are found. Expand your minor II–V–I worksheets to accommodate these new ideas.

Worksheets

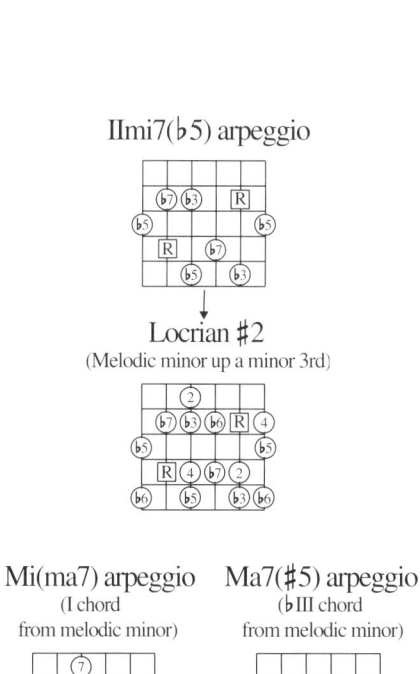

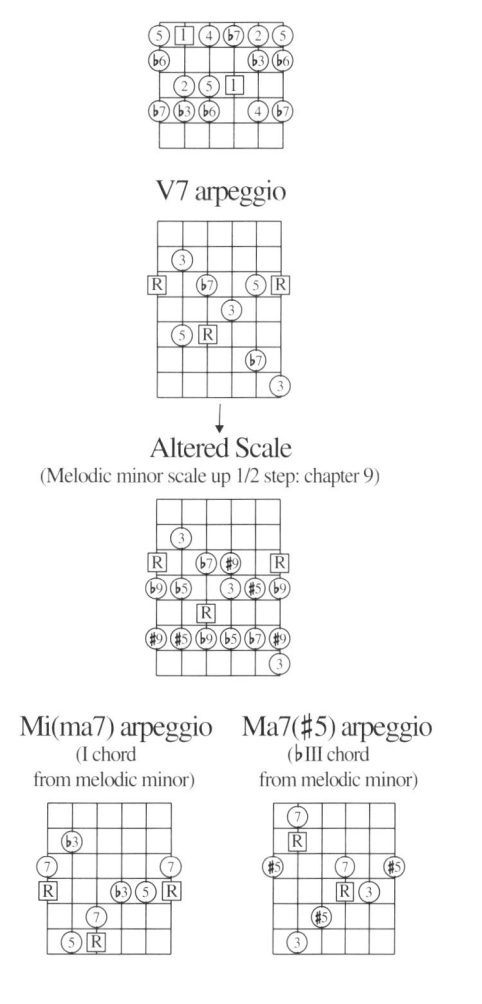

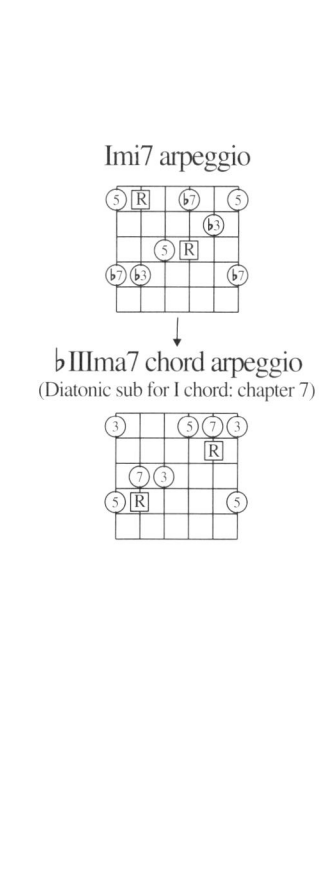

Pattern II Minor Scale

[Fretboard diagram]

IImi7(♭5) arpeggio

[Fretboard diagram]

↓

Locrian ♯2
(Melodic minor up a minor 3rd)

[Fretboard diagram]

Mi(ma7) arpeggio   Ma7(♯5) arpeggio
(I chord   (♭III chord
from melodic minor) from melodic minor)

[Fretboard diagrams]

V7 arpeggio

[Fretboard diagram]

↓

Altered Scale
(Melodic minor scale up 1/2 step: chapter 9)

[Fretboard diagram]

Mi(ma7) arpeggio   Ma7(♯5) arpeggio
(I chord   (♭III chord
from melodic minor) from melodic minor)

[Fretboard diagrams]

Imi7 arpeggio

[Fretboard diagram]

↓

♭IIIma7 chord arpeggio
(Diatonic sub for I chord: chapter 7)

[Fretboard diagram]

Pattern IV Minor Scale

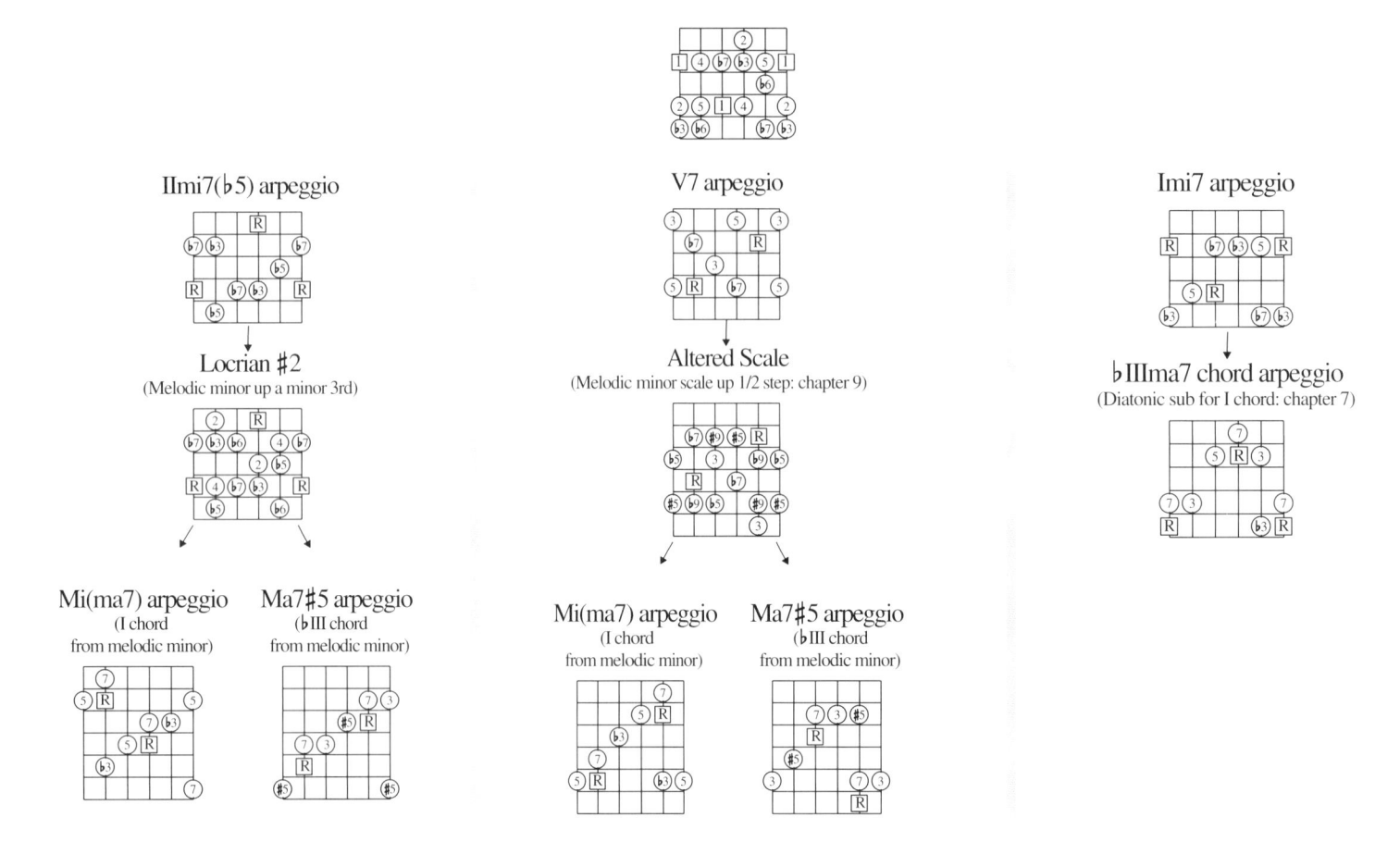

IImi7(♭5) arpeggio

↓

Locrian #2
(Melodic minor up a minor 3rd)

↓   ↓

Mi(ma7) arpeggio   **Ma7♯5 arpeggio**
(I chord   (♭III chord
from melodic minor)   from melodic minor)

V7 arpeggio

↓

Altered Scale
(Melodic minor scale up 1/2 step: chapter 9)

↓   ↓

Mi(ma7) arpeggio   **Ma7♯5 arpeggio**
(I chord   (♭III chord
from melodic minor)   from melodic minor)

Imi7 arpeggio

↓

♭IIIma7 chord arpeggio
(Diatonic sub for I chord: chapter 7)

Let's hear what this type of idea sounds like. Here's a sample lick in the key of C minor using Pattern II. The lick uses an A♭ma7(♯5) arpeggio from F melodic minor over the IImi7(♭5) chord (Dmi7(♭5)), an A♭mi(ma7) arpeggio over the V7 chord (G7), and resolves to the 9th of the I chord.

Track 31

Dmi7(♭5)   G7   Cmi7
A♭ma7(♯5) arpeggio   A♭mi(ma7) arpeggio

Continue writing new licks incorporating your new information.

Chapter 17

Chapter Summary:

- All of the notes of the Locrian ♯2 scale are chord tones and extensions of a mi7(♭5) chord. The notes of the Locrian ♯2 scale are the same as the notes of the melodic minor scale up a minor 3rd. Therefore, all the notes of this melodic minor scale are chord tones of a mi7(♭5) chord with extensions.
- Harmonizing the melodic minor scale (arpeggios) will give us combinations of notes we'll call "combo plates." Focus on using the first and third arpeggios from the harmonized melodic minor scale.
- Add these new arpeggio choices to your worksheets. Be sure they fit within the four- or five-fret span of the scale pattern for the I chord.

What we've covered thus far:

- key center and chord tone soloing
- arpeggio organization in major
- arpeggio organization in minor
- common situation concept
- the arpeggio connecting game
- the arpeggio connecting game in more patterns
- expanding our note options with added color tones
- the melodic minor scale
- adding altered tones
- referencing and worksheets
- the connecting game with the altered scale
- the Locrian ♯2 scale
- writing licks
- inserting licks
- disguising licks
- harmonizing the melodic minor scale for altered dominants
- harmonizing the melodic minor scale for minor 7(♭5) chords

What's next?

- turnaround licks for situations 7 and 8

18 Turnaround Licks in Major (III–VI–II–V–I)

> **Objective:**
> - To learn how to write licks for a major III–VI–II–V–I progression.
> - To learn to expand our worksheets to accommodate a III–VI–II–V–I progression.

Chapters 13–15 have taught us how to write major and minor II–V–I licks as presented in situations 1–4. In this chapter we'll learn to write licks for situations 5 and 6, which are commonly referred to as *turnarounds*.

The Major Turnaround Lick

Where will you see a major III–VI–II–V–I? In blues, we think of the turnaround as the last two measures of a progression that prepare the listener for the beginning of the form again. The turnaround in blues "turns you around" so you can begin again. In a jazz context, the turnaround does the same thing. However, in jazz you might see a turnaround in places other than just the very end of the form. It might be at the end of a section. The turnaround steers the progression back to start on the I chord again. There are other examples where a III–VI–II–V–I might appear at the beginning or middle of a section. But one thing is for sure, the progression is common enough to deserve a spot in our list of eleven common situations.

Before writing any lick, it is important to create a worksheet. When you examine a III–VI–II–V–I, you should recognize that the last three chords are very familiar: II–V–I! That means that creating a III–VI–II–V–I lick worksheet is just a matter of adding IIImi7 and VI7 (with all the altered options) in front of the II–V–I information.

> **Note:**
> The VI7 chord is a functioning *secondary dominant*. It acts as the V of the II chord in the III–VI–II–V–I progression. Because it is functioning, the altered scale (melodic minor up a half step from the root of the dominant) is a good choice. That also allows us to play the combo plate arpeggios from melodic minor that we studied in Chapter 16.
>
> Also, note that IIImi7 is a member of the tonic family (see Chapter 7). Often times, a III–VI–II–V–I is written and seen as I–VI–II–V–I. This slight variation has no real impact on the notes we choose when we write licks for a turnaround. The decision about whether to play III or I is often made spontaneously.

Chapter 18

Worksheets

Pattern I Major

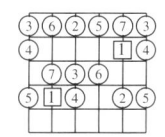

IIImi7 arpeggio 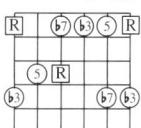 · VI7 arpeggio 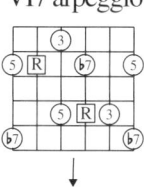 → Altered Scale (Melodic minor scale up 1/2 step: chapter 9) → Mi(ma7) arpeggio (I chord from melodic minor) · Ma7(♯5) arpeggio (♭III chord from melodic minor)

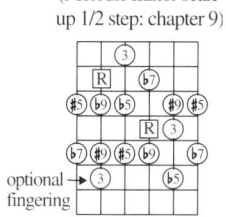

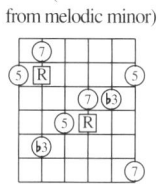

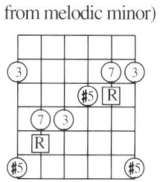

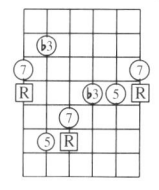

IImi7 arpeggio 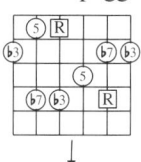 · IVma7 arpeggio (Diatonic sub for II chord)

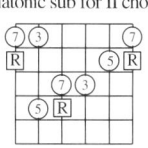

V7 arpeggio 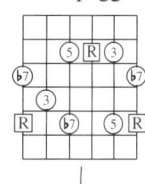 → Altered Scale (Melodic minor scale up 1/2 step: chapter 9) → Mi(ma7) arpeggio (I chord from melodic minor) · Ma7(♯5) arpeggio (♭III chord from melodic minor)

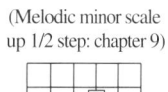

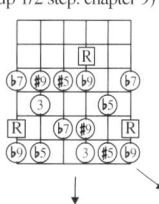

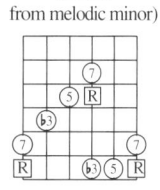

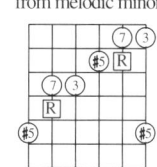

Ima7 arpeggio

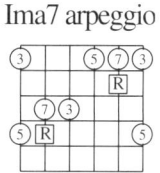

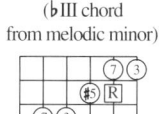

Pattern III Major

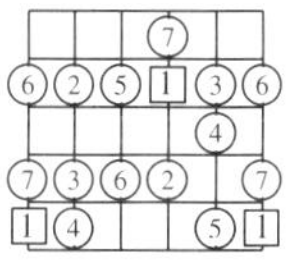

IImi7 arpeggio  · VI7 arpeggio 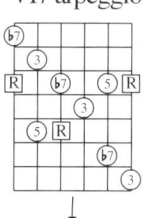 → Altered Scale (Melodic minor scale up 1/2 step) → Mi(ma7) arpeggio (I chord from melodic minor) · Ma7(♯5) arpeggio (♭III chord from melodic minor)

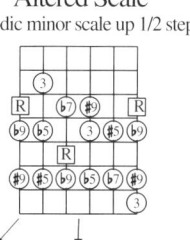

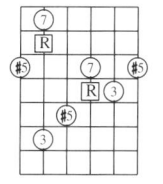

IImi7 arpeggio 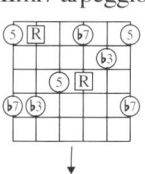 · IVma7 arpeggio (Diatonic Sub for II chord)

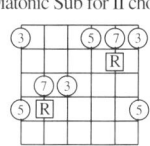

V7 arpeggio 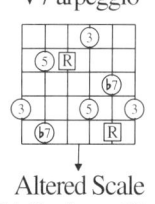 → Altered Scale (Melodic minor up 1/2 step) → Mi(ma7) arpeggio (I chord from melodic minor) · Ma7(♯5) arpeggio (♭III chord from melodic minor)

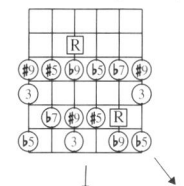

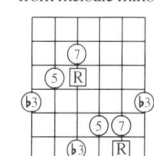

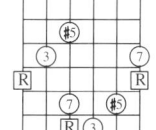

Ima7 arpeggio

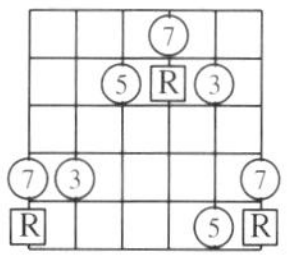

Remember that our ultimate goal is to progress beyond the point of playing licks. We want to be able to express ourselves freely and comfortably. But first, we will devote a lot of time and energy into building up our vocabulary of licks.

Be sure that the first turnaround licks you write are very easy to play. Use simple, steady rhythms and easy fingerings. By keeping things simple, you can easily change and improvise with the phrase in a real solo.

Let's first write a lick for situation #5 (long major III–VI–II–V–I). Look at your Pattern I major III–VI–II–V–I worksheet. We'll write the lick in F major using Pattern I. All of the options we've discussed so far for each of the five chords are at your disposal. You have assembled some very good options for note choices. Use the following rhythmic template.

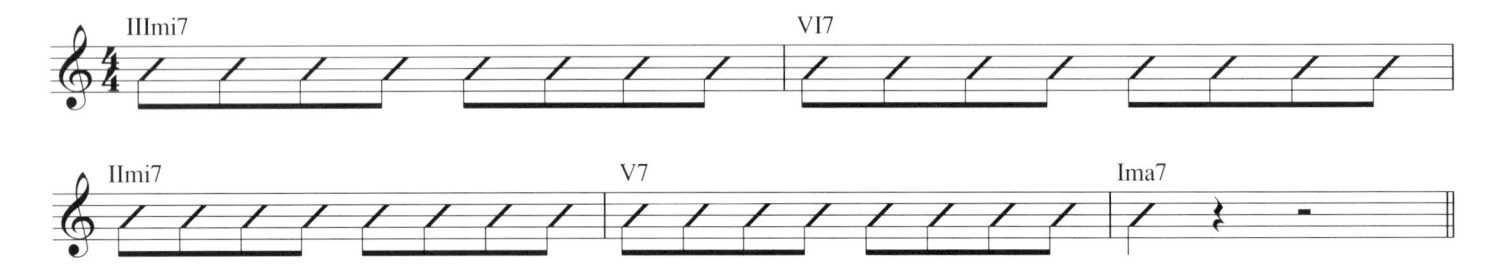

Here's a sample lick in F using the above rhythmic template. My thought process was this:

- Over the III chord, Ami7, I looked at my worksheet and selected the IIImi7 arpeggio (Ami7) and created a melody from those tones.
- Over the VI7 chord, D7, I looked at my worksheet and selected notes from the altered scale combo plate E♭mi(ma7) arpeggio (melodic minor up a half step from the root of the VI7 chord).
- Over the II chord, Gmi7, I looked at my worksheet and selected the IV chord arpeggio (B♭ma7) because it's a good option as discussed in Chapter 7.
- Over the V chord, C7, I looked at the worksheet and selected the C altered scale. I just selected notes of the scale and resolved to the 3rd of the I chord, Fma7.

Track 32

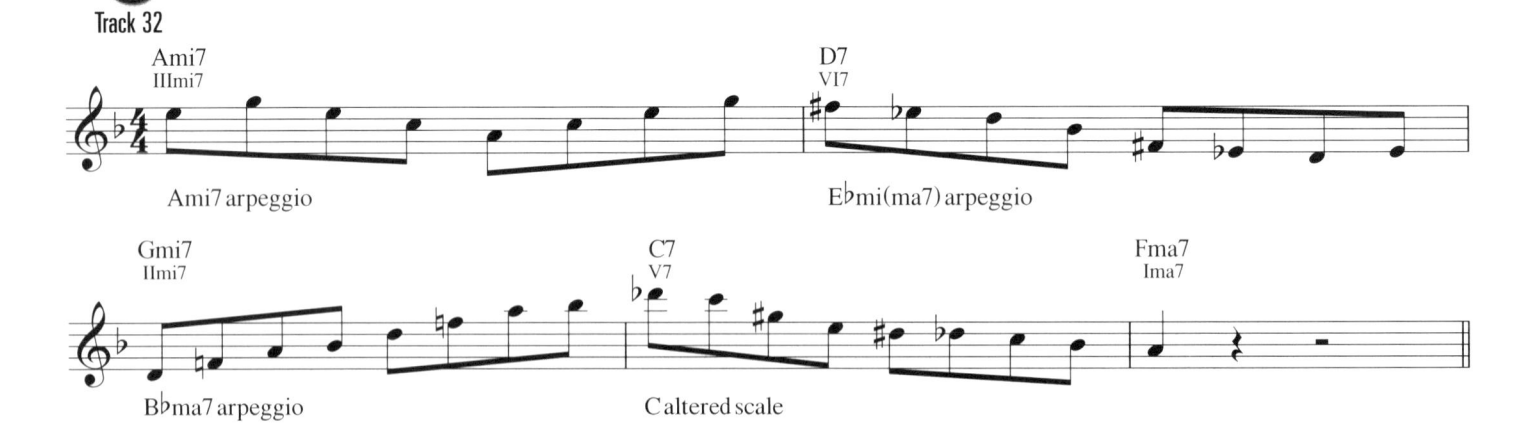

Now we'll write a lick for situation #6 (short major III–VI–II–V–I). Look at your Pattern I major worksheet again. Use the following rhythmic template.

Chapter 18

Here's a sample lick in F using the previous rhythmic template. I used some of the same note choices as the previous lick; I simply shortened the lines to fit the new chord progression.

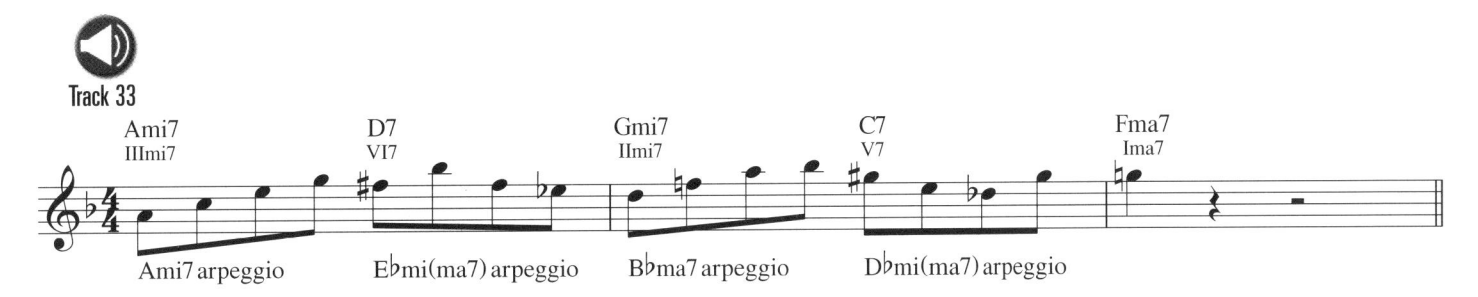

Track 33

Ami7	D7	Gmi7	C7	Fma7
IIImi7	VI7	IImi7	V7	Ima7

Ami7 arpeggio — E♭mi(ma7) arpeggio — B♭ma7 arpeggio — D♭mi(ma7) arpeggio

Now it's your turn to start writing turnaround licks. You now have the tools, so use them! You are now equipped to write licks for the first six common situations. Continue adding chapters to your book of licks you started in Chapter 13. Apply all of the same practice concepts to these new licks as well (using a metronome, moving them to new keys, and inserting them into songs with turnaround progressions).

Variations of the Major Turnaround

There are many reharmonizations of the III–VI–II–V–I. Jazz musicians often reharmonize songs or parts of songs spontaneously. You should familiarize yourself with the considerable list of variations.

1. IIImi7–VImi7–IImi7–V7–Ima7 (Notice that all of the chords are diatonic)
2. IIImi7(♭5)–VI7–IImi7–V7–Ima7
3. IIImi7–♭III7–IImi7–V7–Ima7
4. IIImi7–♭III7–IImi7–♭II7–Ima7
5. III7–VI7–II7–V7–Ima7
6. III7–♭III7–II7–♭II7–Ima7
7. IIImi7(♭5)–VI7–IImi7(♭5)–V7–Ima7

Helpful Hint:

The second progression above presents an interesting scenario that can be very helpful. Let's put the progression in a context—the key of C. It looks like this: Emi7(♭5)–A7–Dmi7–G7–Cma7.

Notice how the first three chords look like a II–V–I in D minor. A very convenient way to construct a turnaround lick is to combine a minor II–V–I lick with a major II–V–I lick. In the key of C, you could combine a Pattern II minor II–V–I lick in D minor with a Pattern III major II–V–I lick in C, and the whole thing would basically fall within the pattern III major shape.

When using your turnaround vocabulary over III–VI–II–V–I variations, tempo is a major factor in how perfectly your licks need to match with the spontaneous reharmonization. If the tempo is very fast, you could play a lick you wrote that fits perfectly over IIImi7–VI7–IImi7–V7 even when the person comping for you plays any of the seven variations listed above. It won't fit perfectly, but the strength of your line will probably make the lick work. The slower the tempo, the more important it is that you adjust your line to the tones of the chords actually being played.

Remember to keep practicing the arpeggio connecting game with our new options. Continue writing new licks that incorporate your new information.

Chapter Summary:

- III–VI–II–V–I chord progressions are very common. Sometimes they appear as I–VI–II–V–I.
- III–VI–II–V–I chord progressions may appear at the end of a song, the end of a section, or in the interior of a section.
- To create a III–VI–II–V–I worksheet, take a II–V–I worksheet and add your III and VI options in front.
- "Store" your licks in a convenient key, but practice them in all keys.
- Be aware of the common variations of the turnaround.
- Build some of your turnaround vocabulary by combining minor and major II–V–I licks.

What we've covered thus far:

- key center and chord tone soloing
- arpeggio organization in major
- arpeggio organization in minor
- common situation concept
- the arpeggio connecting game
- the arpeggio connecting game in more patterns
- expanding our note options with added color tones
- the melodic minor scale
- adding altered tones
- referencing and worksheets
- the connecting game with the altered scale
- the Locrian ♯2 scale
- writing licks
- inserting licks
- disguising licks
- harmonizing the melodic minor scale for altered dominants
- harmonizing the melodic minor scale for minor 7(♭5) chords
- turnaround licks in major (III–VI–II–V–I)

What's next:

- turnaround licks in minor (I–VI–II–V–I)

19 Turnaround Licks in Minor (I–IV–II–V–I)

> **Objective:**
> - To learn how to write licks for a minor I–VI–II–V–I progression.
> - To learn to expand our minor II–V–I worksheets to accommodate a minor I–VI–II–V–I progression.

We learned how to write major turnaround licks in Chapter 18. In this chapter we'll learn to write turnaround licks in a minor key. These will apply to situations 7 and 8, long and short minor turnarounds (I–VI–II–V–I), respectively.

The Minor Turnaround Lick

Where will you see a minor I–VI–II–V–I? You see them in most of the same places as you do major turnaround licks. The end of a blues is a common place. you'll also find them at the end, middle, or beginning of a section in jazz standards. It's certainly common enough to deserve a spot in our list of eleven common situations.

Before writing any lick, creating a worksheet for that lick-type is important. When you examine a minor I–VI–II–V–I (minor turnaround), you should recognize that its last three chords are something very familiar: a minor II–V–I! That means creating a minor turnaround lick worksheet is just a matter of adding Imi7 and VImi7(♭5) with all the color options in front of the II–V–I information on a minor II–V–I worksheet. This is the same idea we used in Chapter 18 when building major turnaround licks.

Please note that VImi7(♭5) can use a Locrian ♯2 sound. Because a minor 7(♭5) chord begs for the Locrian ♯2 sound, melodic minor up minor 3rd from the root of the mi7(♭5) chord) is a good choice. That also allows us to play the combo plate arpeggios from melodic minor.

> **Helpful Hint:**
> Notice that in a minor turnaround, the Locrian ♯2 scale used over the VI chord is simply the melodic minor scale of the key. For example, over Ami7(♭5) in the key of C minor, where Ami7(♭5) is the VI chord, the A Locrian ♯2 scale is the same scale as C melodic minor.

Worksheets

Pattern II Minor

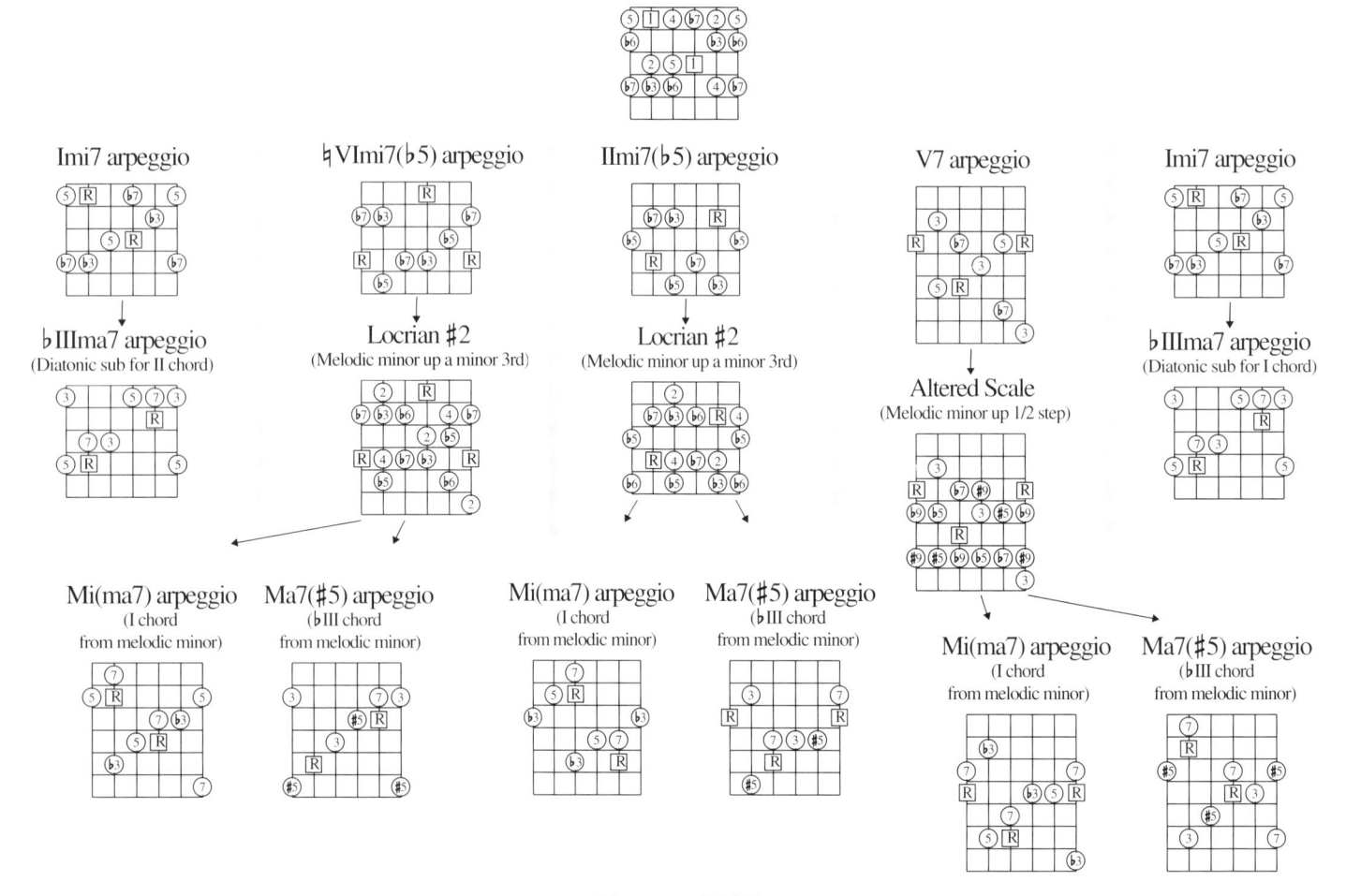

Imi7 arpeggio | **♮VImi7(♭5) arpeggio** | **IImi7(♭5) arpeggio** | **V7 arpeggio** | **Imi7 arpeggio**

♭IIIma7 arpeggio
(Diatonic sub for II chord)

Locrian #2
(Melodic minor up a minor 3rd)

Locrian #2
(Melodic minor up a minor 3rd)

Altered Scale
(Melodic minor up 1/2 step)

♭IIIma7 arpeggio
(Diatonic sub for I chord)

Mi(ma7) arpeggio
(I chord from melodic minor)

Ma7(#5) arpeggio
(♭III chord from melodic minor)

Mi(ma7) arpeggio
(I chord from melodic minor)

Ma7(#5) arpeggio
(♭III chord from melodic minor)

Mi(ma7) arpeggio
(I chord from melodic minor)

Ma7(#5) arpeggio
(♭III chord from melodic minor)

Pattern IV Minor

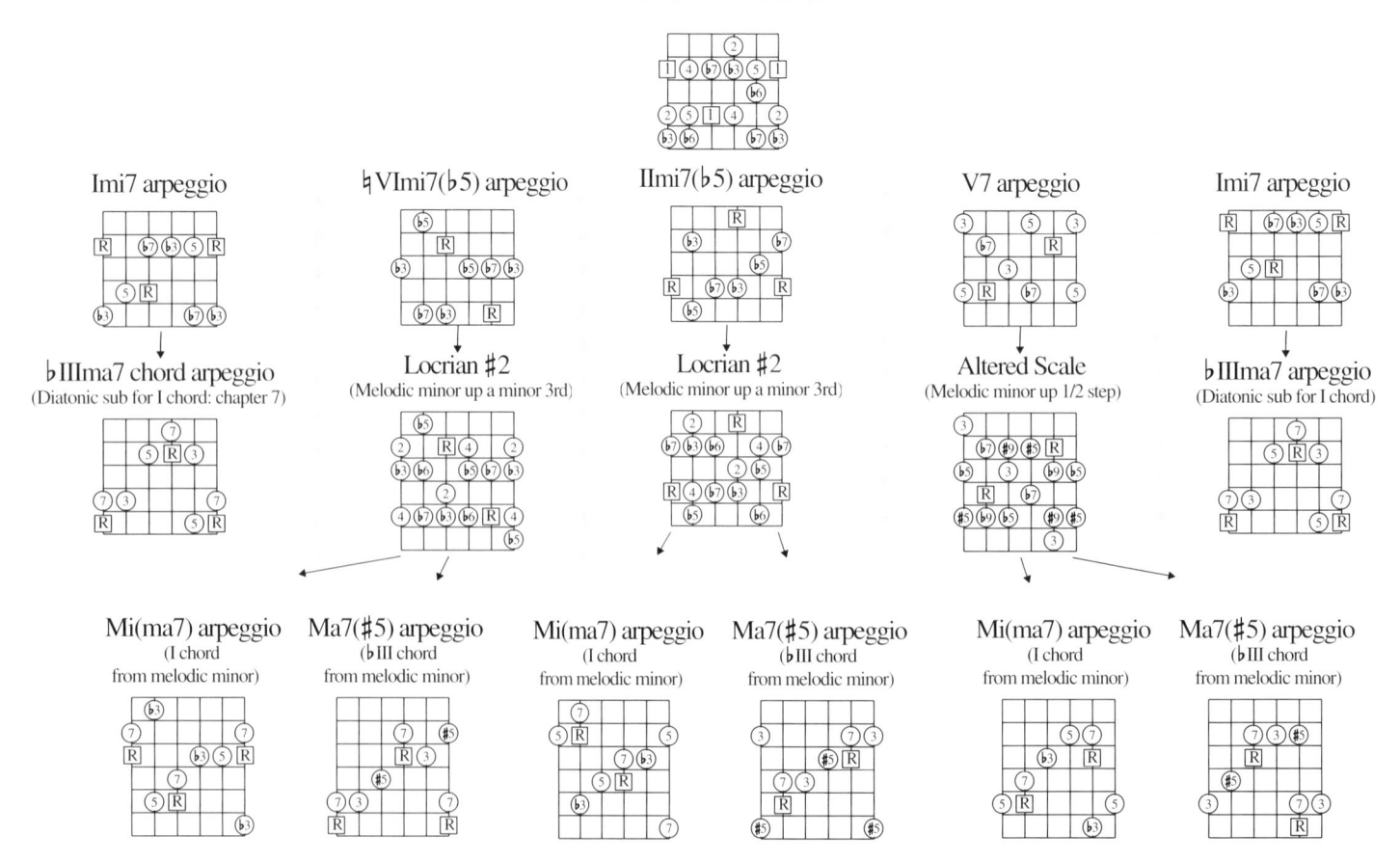

Imi7 arpeggio | **♮VImi7(♭5) arpeggio** | **IImi7(♭5) arpeggio** | **V7 arpeggio** | **Imi7 arpeggio**

♭IIIma7 chord arpeggio
(Diatonic sub for I chord: chapter 7)

Locrian #2
(Melodic minor up a minor 3rd)

Locrian #2
(Melodic minor up a minor 3rd)

Altered Scale
(Melodic minor up 1/2 step)

♭IIIma7 arpeggio
(Diatonic sub for I chord)

Mi(ma7) arpeggio
(I chord from melodic minor)

Ma7(#5) arpeggio
(♭III chord from melodic minor)

Mi(ma7) arpeggio
(I chord from melodic minor)

Ma7(#5) arpeggio
(♭III chord from melodic minor)

Mi(ma7) arpeggio
(I chord from melodic minor)

Ma7(#5) arpeggio
(♭III chord from melodic minor)

Chapter 19

Remember that the first minor I–VI–II–V–I licks you write should be very easy to play using simple, steady rhythms and easy fingerings. First we'll write a lick for situation #7 (long minor I–VI–II–V–I). Look at your Pattern II minor worksheet. All of the options we've discussed so far for each of the five chords are at your disposal. You have assembled some very good options for note choices. Use the following rhythmic template for your licks.

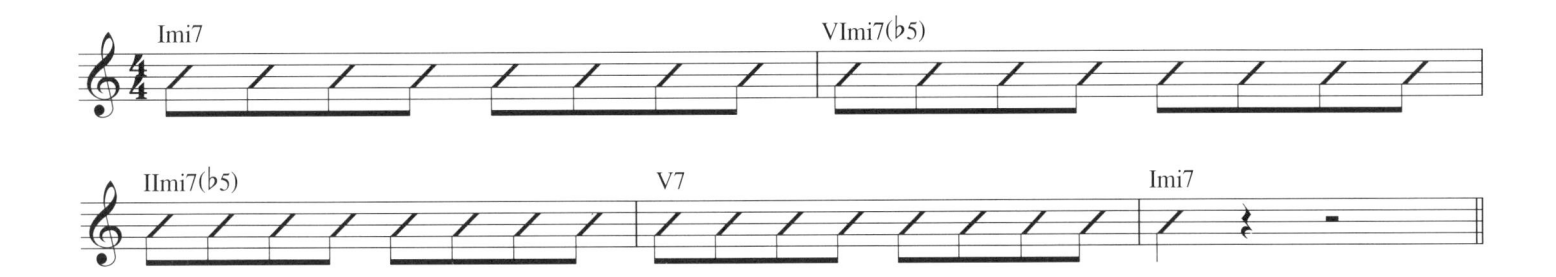

Here's a sample lick in C minor using the above rhythmic template. My thought process was this:

- Over the I chord, Cmi7, I looked at my worksheet, selected the C minor scale, and created a melody from those tones.
- Over the VImi7(♭5) chord, Ami7(♭5), I looked at my worksheet and selected notes from the A Locrian ♮2 scale (an E♭ma7(♯5) arpeggio).
- Over the IImi7(♭♭5) chord, Dmi7(♭5), I looked at my worksheet and selected notes from the D Locrian ♮2 scale (an A♭ma7(♯5) arpeggio).
- Over the V7 chord, G7, I looked at my worksheet, selected notes from the G altered scale (an A♭mi(ma7) arpeggio), and resolved to the 9th of the I chord, Cmi7.

Track 34

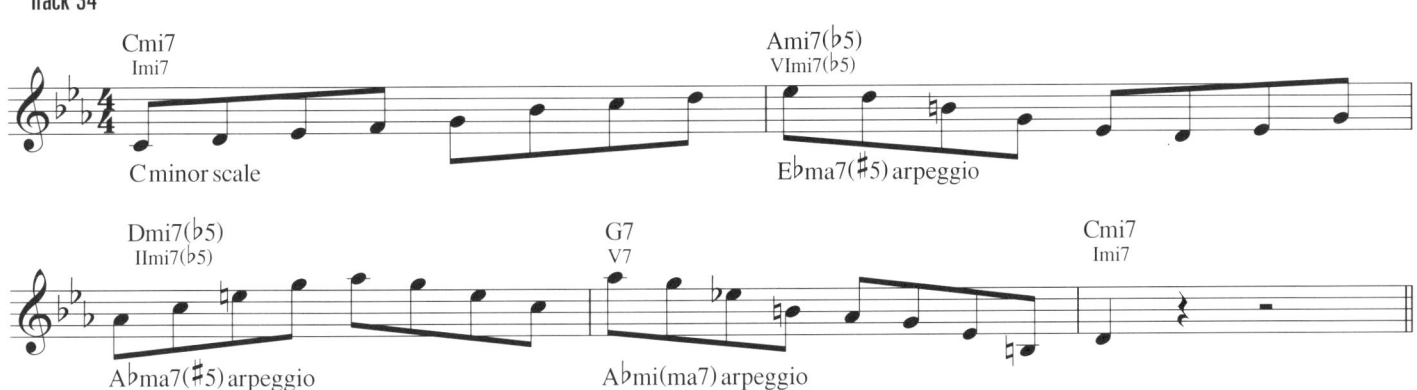

Next we'll write a lick for situation #8 (short minor I–VI–II–V–I). Look at your Pattern II minor worksheet again. Use the following rhythmic template.

Here's a sample lick in C minor using the previous rhythmic template. I used the same thought process as the previous lick; I simply shortened the lines to fit the new chord progression.

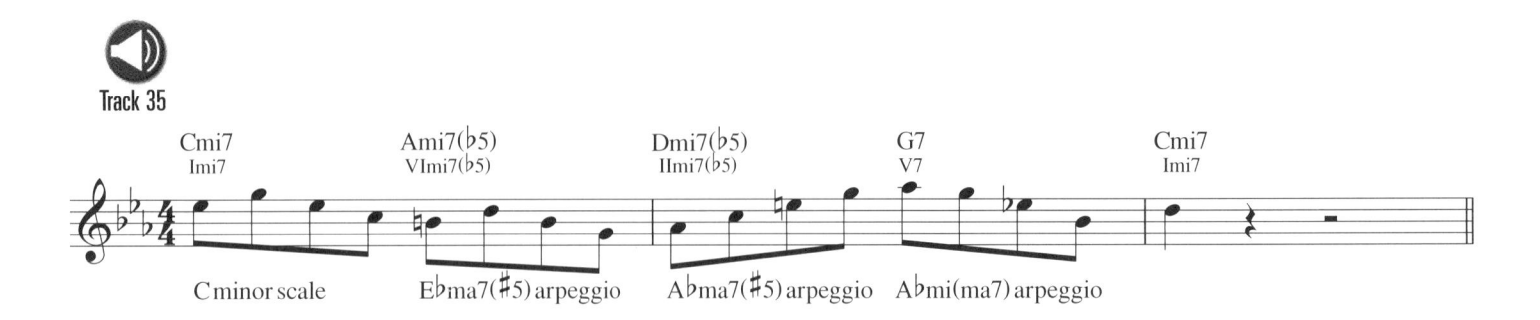

Track 35

Cmi7 / Imi7 — C minor scale
Ami7(♭5) / VImi7(♭5) — E♭ma7(♯5) arpeggio
Dmi7(♭5) / IImi7(♭5) — A♭ma7(♯5) arpeggio
G7 / V7 — A♭mi(ma7) arpeggio
Cmi7 / Imi7

Now it's your turn to start writing licks. You now have the tools, so use them! You are now equipped to write licks for the first eight common situations. Continue adding chapters to your book of licks you started in Chapter 13. Apply all of the same practice concepts to these new licks as well (using a metronome, moving them to new keys, and inserting them into songs with turnaround progressions).

Variations on the Minor Turnaround

There are many reharmonizations of the minor I–VI–II–V–I. Jazz musicians often reharmonize songs or parts of songs spontaneously. You should familiarize yourself with the considerable list of variations.

1. Imi7–♭VIma7–IImi7(♭5)–V7–Imi7
2. Imi7–VImi7(♭5)–II7–V7–Imi7
3. Imi7–♭III7–II7–V7–Imi7
4. Imi7–♭III7–II7–♭II7–Imi7
5. Imi7–♭III7–♭VI7–V7–Imi7
6. Imi7–♭III7–♭VI7–♭II7–Imi7

When using your turnaround vocabulary over minor I–VI–II–V–I variations, tempo is a major factor in how perfectly your licks need to match with the "spontaneous reharmonization." If the tempo is very fast, you could play a lick that fits perfectly over Imi7–VImi7(♭5)–IImi7(♭5)–V7–Imi7 even when the person comping for you plays any of the six variations listed above. It won't fit perfectly, but the strength of your line will probably make the lick work. The slower the tempo, the more important it is that you adjust your line to the notes of the chords actually being played.

Remember to keep practicing the arpeggio connecting game with our new options. Continue writing new licks that incorporate your new information.

Chapter 19

Chapter Summary:

- Minor I–VI–II–V–I chord progressions are very common.
- Minor I–VI–II–V–I chord progressions may appear at the end of a song, the end of a section, or in the interior of a section.
- To create a minor I–VI–II–V–I worksheet, take your II–V–I worksheet and add your I and VI options in front.
- "Store" your licks in a convenient key, but practice them in all keys.
- Be aware of the common variations of the minor turnaround..

What we've covered thus far:

- key center and chord tone soloing
- arpeggio organization in major
- arpeggio organization in minor
- common situation concept
- the arpeggio connecting game
- the arpeggio connecting game in more patterns
- expanding our note options with added color tones
- the melodic minor scale
- adding altered tones
- referencing and worksheets
- the connecting game with the altered scale
- the Locrian ♯2 scale
- writing licks
- inserting licks
- disguising licks
- harmonizing the melodic minor scale for altered dominants
- harmonizing the melodic minor scale for minor 7(♭5) chords
- turnaround licks in major (III–VI–II–V–I)
- turnaround licks in minor (I–VI–II–V–I)

What's next:

- the Lydian ♭7 scale

The Lydian ♭7 Scale

20

> **Objective:**
> - To learn the use of Lydian ♭7 over non-functioning dominant 7th chords.

Non-Functioning Dominant 7th Chords

In Chapter 9, we studied functioning dominant 7th chords—i.e., dominant chords that resolve to their respective I chord. In this chapter we'll take a look at the other type of dominants: *non-functioning*.

When a dominant chord does not resolve to its I chord, the harmony doesn't act the way we expect. Therefore, the scale choice for a non-functioning should not be one that sets up expectations of a I chord. We need a scale choice that will not make the listener feel that the I chord is coming; that scale is the Lydian ♭7 scale. Its formula is 1–2–3–♯4–5–6–♭7. Notice that all four tones of the dominant 7th are present: 1, 3, 5, and ♭7.

> **Helpful Hint:**
> Try looking at scales as arpeggios with notes in between chord tones. Notice that the 2nd (9th) is between 1 and 3, the ♯4th (♯11) is between 3 and 5, and the 6th (13th) is between 5 and

What is it about the Lydian ♭7 scale that softens the strong attraction to the I chord? The ♯11. The ♯11 is a "disorienting tone" that seems to give the entire Lydian ♭7 scale an ambiguous effect.

The Melodic Minor Connection

In Chapter 8, we learned that the modes of the melodic minor scale are more useful than the scale itself for use as chord scales over different chords. We learned the seventh mode of the melodic minor scale, which is also known as the altered scale or the Super Locrian. We've also learned the sixth mode of melodic minor is identical to the Locrian ♯2 scale. In this chapter we'll find another melodic minor connection in relation to the Lydian ♭7 scale.

Here are the notes of the G Lydian ♭7 scale.

G Lydian ♭7

| R | 9 | 3 | ♯11 | 5 | 13 | ♭7 |
| (1) | (2) | | (♯4) | | (6) | |

And here are the notes of a D melodic minor scale.

D melodic minor

Chapter 20

A side-by-side comparison shows the amazing coincidence.

G Lydian ♭7

D melodic minor

They're the same notes! We can say that the G Lydian ♭7 scale is the same as playing the D melodic minor scale from the 4th degree to the 4th degree. This means that G Lydian ♭7 is another name for the fourth mode of D melodic minor. Put yet another way, we can say that the G Lydian ♭7 scale is the same as playing the melodic minor scale up a 5th from the root of the non-functioning dominant 7th chord. For now, we will rely on this way of explaining the Lydian ♭7 scale/melodic minor scale relationship.

So, over a non-functioning dominant 7th chord, in order to soften the sense of pull to the I chord and create a feeling of ambiguity, you may play the Lydian ♭7 scale from the root of the V dominant 7th chord. This is the same as playing the melodic minor scale up a 5th from the root of the V dominant 7th chord.

G7 chord   G7 arpeggio   G Lydian ♭7 Scale   D melodic minor   D melodic minor with G7 chord tones shaded

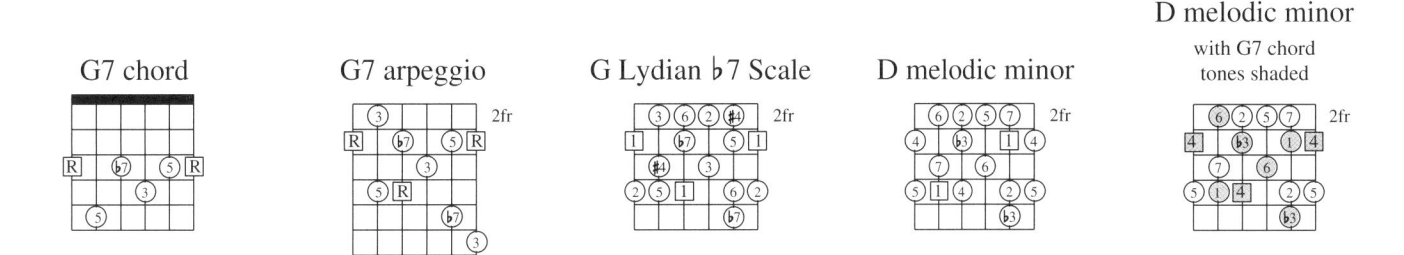

Track 36 — Listen to the CD example of the static G7 chord and the G Lydian ♭7 scale (D melodic minor scale) being applied.

Track 37 — Now you try playing the G Lydian ♭7 scale over the static G7 vamp.

Clearly not all non-functioning dominant 7th chords are static vamps. Most will be found surrounded by other chords. The next example puts the non-functioning G7 chord in a short progression with another chord. Listen to the CD example. Ama7 is the tonic chord, therefore we use the A major scale over it. Since the G7 is therefore a non-functioning dominant, we use G Lydian ♭7 (D melodic minor scale) over it.

Track 38 — Ama7 | G7

73

Now you try it playing over the same backing track using the previously explained scales.

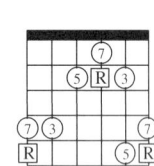

Track 39

Ama7

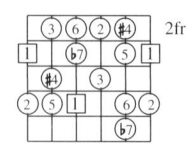

G Lydian ♭7
(D melodic minor)

We've now looked at a non-resolving dominant 7th chord in two ways: as a static vamp and in a simple cyclic progression. Chapter 22 will explore situations 9 and 10: non-resolving II–V progressions.

Chapter Summary:

- All dominant 7th chords can be divided into two groups: functioning and non-functioning. Functioning dominants resolve to their I chord, and non-functioning dominants do not.
- The Lydian ♭7 scale is an appropriate scale for non-functioning dominants because it will not make the listener feel that the I chord is coming.
- The Lydian ♭7 scale is the same as playing the melodic minor scale up a 5th from the root of the non-functioning dominant 7th chord.

What we've covered thus far:

- key center and chord tone soloing
- arpeggio organization in major
- arpeggio organization in minor
- common situation concept
- the arpeggio connecting game
- the arpeggio connecting game in more patterns
- expanding our note options with added color tones
- the melodic minor scale
- adding altered tones
- referencing and worksheets
- the connecting game with the altered scale
- the Locrian ♯2 scale
- writing licks
- inserting licks
- disguising licks
- harmonizing the melodic minor scale for altered dominants
- harmonizing the melodic minor scale for minor 7(♭5) chords
- turnaround licks in major (III–VI–II–V–I)
- turnaround licks in minor (I–VI–II–V–I)
- the Lydian ♭7 scale

What's next:

- harmonizing the melodic minor scale for non-functioning dominants

21 Harmonizing the Melodic Minor Scale for Non-Functioning Dominants

> **Objective:**
> - To expand our use of the melodic minor scale.
> - To learn to use the arpeggios created by harmonizing the melodic minor scale for non-functioning dominant 7th chords.

In Chapters 16 and 17 we harmonized the melodic minor scale for use over altered dominants (the altered scale) and minor 7(♭5) chords (the Locrian ♮2 scale), respectively. We learned to use these note combinations (combo plates) as a source of ideas in creating the "V part" of our II–V–I licks and the "IImi7(♭5) part" of our minor II–V–I licks.

In Chapter 20 we learned about the Lydian ♭7 scale and how it can be used over a non-functioning dominant 7th chord. We learned the connection between Lydian ♭7 and the melodic minor scale up a 5th from the root of the non-functioning dominant 7th chord. In this chapter we'll apply the same "combo plate" principal to the melody-menu that is the Lydian ♭7 application of the melodic minor scale. Examine the numbers below.

G Lydian ♭7:

G	A	B	C♯	D	E	F
1	2 (9)	3	♯4 (♯11)	5	6 (13)	♭7

D Melodic Minor Scale: D   E   F   G   A   B   C♯
(up a 5th from G)

Remember that the G Lydian ♭7 scale contains the same notes as D melodic minor scale. The G Lydian ♭7 scale is the "menu." Therefore, the melodic minor scale up a 5th from the root of the non-functioning dominant7th chord is the same menu. If we agree to say that every note in the Lydian ♭7 scale is a chord tone, then it's safe to say that any combination of notes we choose to play from the menu will be made up of chord tones. Harmonizing the melodic minor scale (arpeggios) might show us combinations of notes we might not have thought about.

Let's put this into context. Here's a static vamp on a non-functioning G7 chord.

We already learned in Chapter 20 that over this G7 chord we could choose the G Lydian ♭7 scale, which is the same as D melodic minor. Now let's look at the arpeggios created when the D melodic minor scale is harmonized and examine what each tone represents relative to the G7 chord.

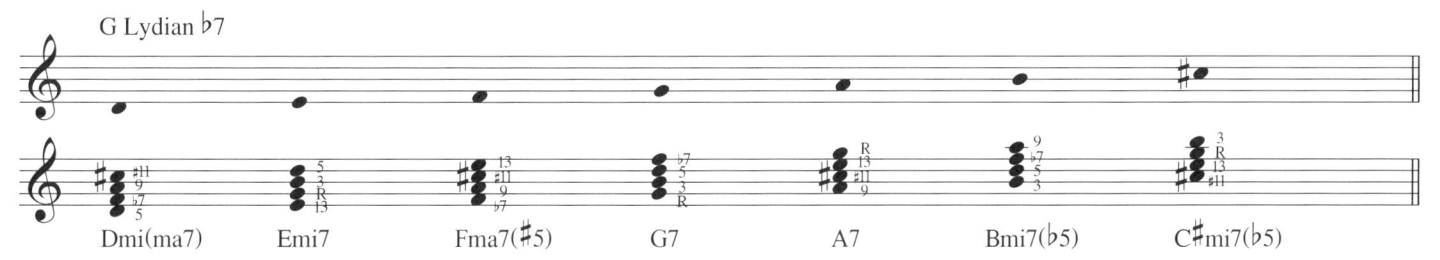

G Lydian ♭7

Dmi(ma7)   Emi7   Fma7(♯5)   G7   A7   Bmi7(♭5)   C♯mi7(♭5)

21

All seven of these arpeggios are viable note combinations (combo plates) of the Lydian ♭7 menu. Most of us would never dream of playing a Dmi(ma7) arpeggio or Fma7(♯5) arpeggio over a G7. Those ideas just wouldn't come to mind. We're introduced to these ideas only because we learned about harmonizing the melodic minor scale.

Work one or two "combo plates" over a static dominant 7th chord and in the progressions from chapter 19. I suggest starting with the first and third arpeggios: the mi(ma7) and the ma7(♯5). The following worksheet shows how the connection is made in relation to a D7 chord.

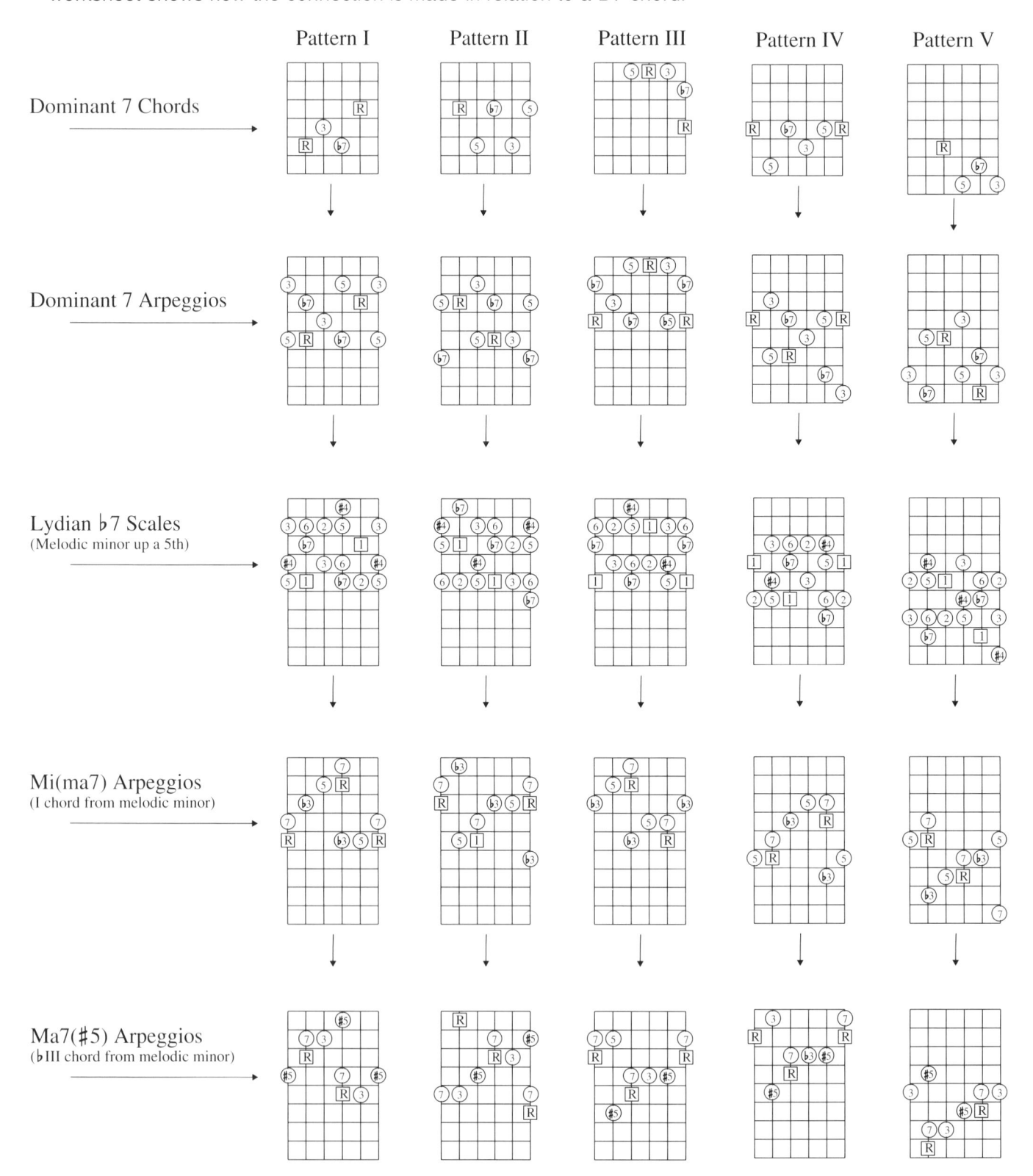

	Pattern I	Pattern II	Pattern III	Pattern IV	Pattern V
Dominant 7 Chords →					
Dominant 7 Arpeggios →					
Lydian ♭7 Scales (Melodic minor up a 5th) →					
Mi(ma7) Arpeggios (I chord from melodic minor) →					
Ma7(♯5) Arpeggios (♭III chord from melodic minor) →					

Chapter 21

🔊 **Track 40** Listen to the CD example of the static G7 chord and the Dmi(ma7) arpeggio (from the D melodic minor scale) being applied.

🔊 **Track 41** Now, you play along with the same track.

Chapter Summary:

- All of the notes of the Lydian ♭7 scale are chord tones of a non-functioning dominant 7th chord (essential chord tones and extensions). The notes of the Lydian ♭7 scale are the same as the notes of the melodic minor scale up a 5th. Therefore, all the notes of this melodic minor scale are chord tones of a non-functioning dominant 7th chord.
- Harmonizing the melodic minor scale (arpeggios) will give us combinations of notes we'll call "combo plates." Focus on using the first and third arpeggios from the harmonized melodic minor scale.
- Add these new arpeggios choices to your worksheets. Be sure they fit within the four- or five-fret span of the scale pattern for the I chord.

What we've covered thus far:

- key center and chord tone soloing
- arpeggio organization in major
- arpeggio organization in minor
- common situation concept
- the arpeggio connecting game
- the arpeggio connecting game in more patterns
- expanding our note options with added color tones
- the melodic minor scale
- adding altered tones
- referencing and worksheets
- the connecting game with the altered scale
- the Locrian ♯2 scale
- writing licks
- inserting licks
- disguising licks
- harmonizing the melodic minor scale for altered dominants
- harmonizing the melodic minor scale for minor 7(♭5) chords
- turnaround licks in major (III–VI–II–V–I)
- turnaround licks in minor (I–VI–II–V–I)
- the Lydian ♭7 scale
- harmonizing the melodic minor scale for non-functioning dominants

What's next:

- Non-resolving II–V progressions

22 Non-Resolving II–V Progressions

> **Objective:**
> - To learn to recognize and play over non-resolving II–V progressions (situations 9 and 10).
> - To learn the most common ways non-resolving II–V progressions appear in jazz standards.

In Chapter 4 we learned about the eleven common situations. Situations 1 and 2 look very similar to situations 9 and 10. However, situations 9 and 10 are non-resolving II–V progressions.

Compare situations 1 and 9:

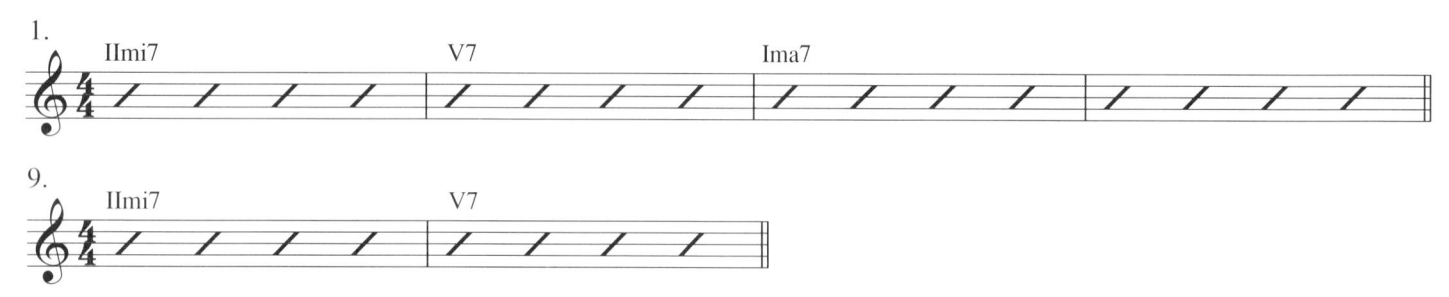

1. | IImi7 | V7 | Ima7 | |

9. | IImi7 | V7 |

Compare situations 2 and 10:

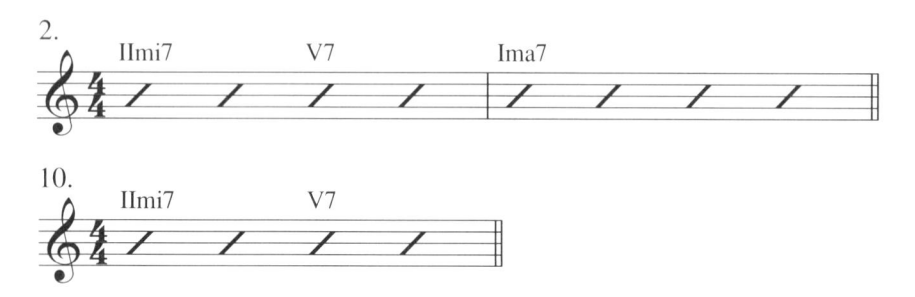

2. | IImi7   V7 | Ima7 |

10. | IImi7   V7 |

We make the distinction between a II–V–I and a non-resolving II–V because of the difference in the dominant 7th chords. In a II–V–I, the dominant 7th chord is functioning, which allows us to play the altered scale plus all of the arpeggios from the melodic minor found scale a half step up from its root.

In a non-resolving II–V, the dominant chord is non-functioning, making the altered scale an inappropriate chord scale choice. For a non-resolving II–V, the appropriate chord scale choice for the dominant chord is the Lydian ♭7, which we studied in Chapters 20 and 21.

There are two parts to our study of non-resolving II–V progressions:

- the note choices available to us
- the most common ways they appear in songs

Chapter 22

First let's talk about what note choices are most commonly used. We'll use situation #9 for study purposes. We'll use Dmi7–G7 for our example.

```
Dmi7            G7
IImi7           V7
```

In this non-resolving II–V, the G7 is a non-functioning dominant, making G Lydian ♭7 (or D melodic minor) the appropriate scale choice. This makes all of the arpeggios from the harmonized D melodic minor scale options as well. The logical arpeggio and scale choices are listed below.

Dmi7 options:

D Dorian
Dmi7 arpeggio
Fma7 arpeggio (diatonic sub)

G7 options:

G Lydian ♭7 (D melodic minor)
Dmi(ma7) arpeggio
Fma7(♯5) arpeggio

The scale options listed above are in that particular order for a reason. The difference between any option under the Dmi7 category differs only by one note from the same option under the G7 category. Let's examine more closely.

If you play D Dorian over the Dmi7 and D melodic minor (G Lydian ♭7) over the G7, only one note changes. D Dorian contains a C♮, and D melodic minor contains a C♯. It's great to exploit both the similarities in the two scales as well as the single note that changes.

If you play a Dmi7 arpeggio over the Dmi7 and a Dmi(ma7) arpeggio (from G Lydian ♭7) over the G7, you have the same one-note difference: C♮ to C♯.

If you play an Fma7 arpeggio over the Dmi7 (diatonic sub) and an Fma7(♯5) arpeggio (from G Lydian ♭7) over the G7, you still have the same one-note difference. The Fma7 arpeggio contains a C♮, and the Fma7(♯5) arpeggio contains a C♯.

🔊 Listen to the CD example.
Track 42

🔊 Now practice with the minus-one track.
Track 43

The most common ways non-resolving II–V progressions appear in songs is the other area of this topic for us to study. After playing a lot of jazz standards, we begin to associate certain chords with others because they appear together so often. We see so many three-chord combinations of II–V–I that it isn't long before we see them as a kind of family unit. The recognition of these associations becomes so strong that when we see the "Dmi7–G7" part of a II–V–I in C (Dmi7–G7–Cma7) we might say, "that's a II–V in C." If feels perfectly natural to see Dmi7–G7 as a II–V even if there's no I chord. Musicians frequently use the term "II–V" for these common companions even if they are not actually II–V of any I chord found in the tune. It's also important to point out that sometimes non-resolving II–Vs are resolving to a I chord at some point in the tune; they just don't immediately resolve to I. **Regardless of how they appear in songs, the note choices we discussed at the start of this chapter are applicable.**

Let's look at how these sometimes "misnamed" II–V progressions appear in songs.

IVmi7–♭VII7

Examine this progression.

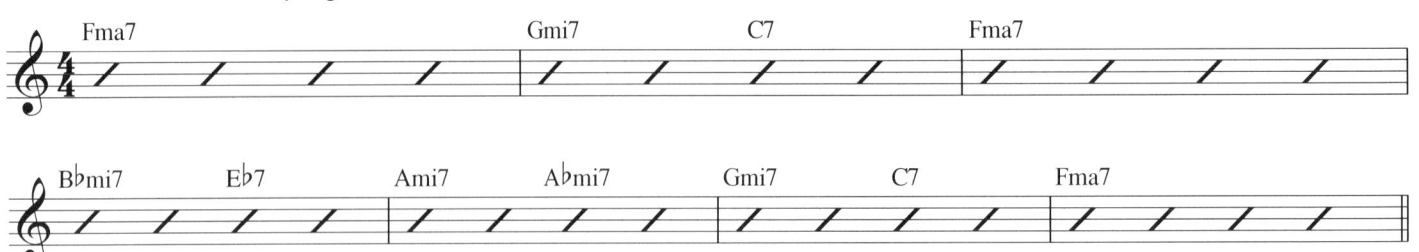

[Fma7 | Gmi7 C7 | Fma7 |]
[B♭mi7 E♭7 | Ami7 A♭mi7 | Gmi7 C7 | Fma7 ||]

There are a few chord combinations in this progression that seem like the II–V combinations described earlier in this chapter: Gmi7–C7, B♭mi7–E♭7, etc. However, if you analyze this progression correctly, it looks like this:

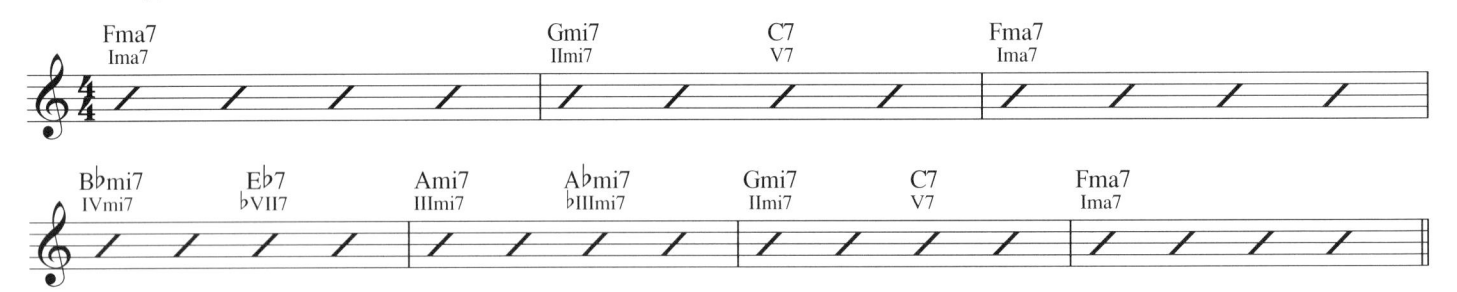

[Fma7 (Ima7) | Gmi7 (IImi7) C7 (V7) | Fma7 (Ima7) |]
[B♭mi7 (IVmi7) E♭7 (♭VII7) | Ami7 (IIImi7) A♭mi7 (♭IIImi7) | Gmi7 (IImi7) C7 (V7) | Fma7 (Ima7) ||]

Notice that the B♭mi7–E♭7 combination is really analyzed as IVmi7–♭VII7—an example of *modal interchange*, or the borrowing of chords from the parallel minor key. This is a very common chord combination to see in a jazz standard. At first glance, an improviser might label this combination as a "II–V in A♭." Regardless of the analysis, it's a classic example of a non-resolving II–V, and the note options we've discussed are perfectly applicable.

Truly Non-Resolving II–V

Here we have a non-resolving II–V (Gmi7–C7) as an actual II–V of the key; there's just no I chord at first. This is truly "II–V" non-resolving. The note options we've discussed are applicable.

Let's look at another progression.

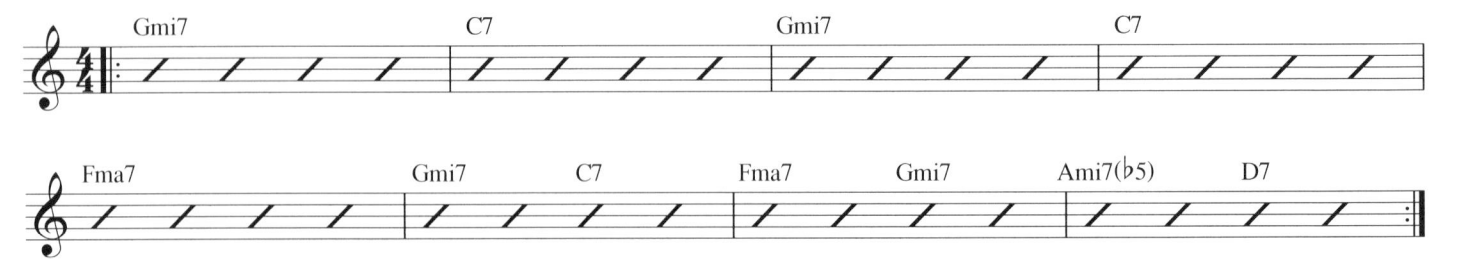

[: Gmi7 | C7 | Gmi7 | C7 |]
[Fma7 | Gmi7 C7 | Fma7 | Gmi7 Ami7(♭5) D7 :]

When you analyze this progression correctly, it looks like this:

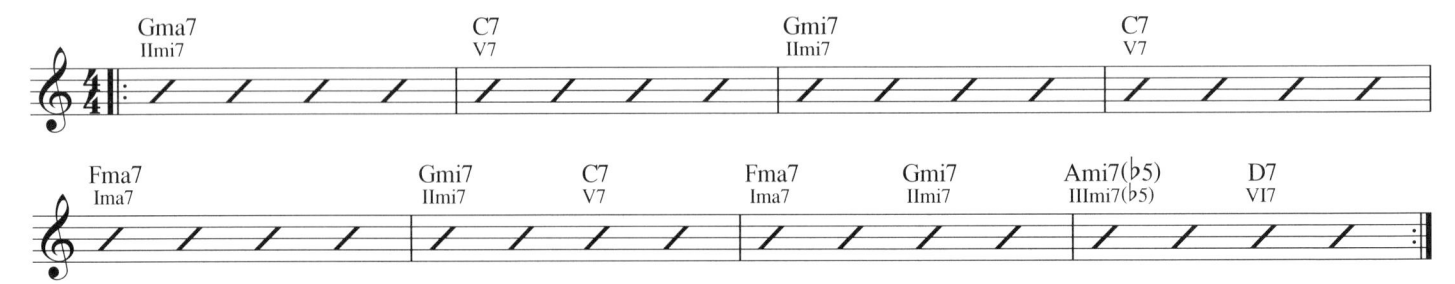

[Gma7 (IImi7) | C7 (V7) | Gmi7 (IImi7) | C7 (V7) |]
[Fma7 (Ima7) | Gmi7 (IImi7) C7 (V7) | Fma7 (Ima7) | Gmi7 (IImi7) Ami7(♭5) (IIImi7(♭5)) D7 (VI7) :]

This next progression contains five different examples:
- VII(♭5)–III7 (II–V of VI)
- Vmi7–I7 (II–V of IV)
- IV7sus–IV7
- IIImi7(♭5)–VII7 (min II–V of II)
- VImi7–II7 (II–V of V)

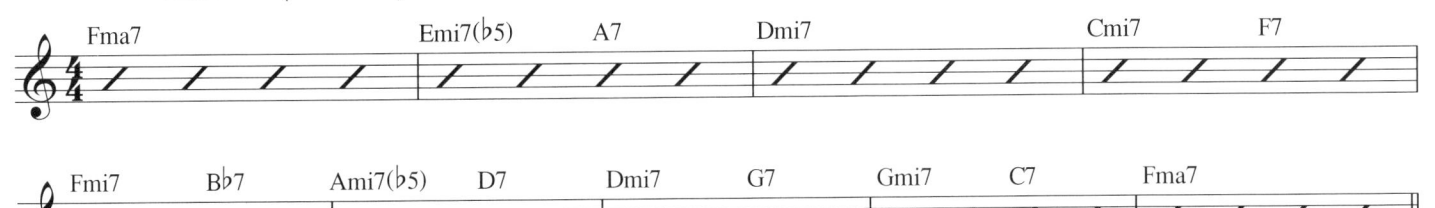

| Fma7 | | Emi7(♭5) | A7 | Dmi7 | | Cmi7 | F7 |

| Fmi7 | B♭7 | Ami7(♭5) | D7 | Dmi7 | G7 | Gmi7 | C7 | Fma7 |

If you analyze this progression correctly, it looks like this:

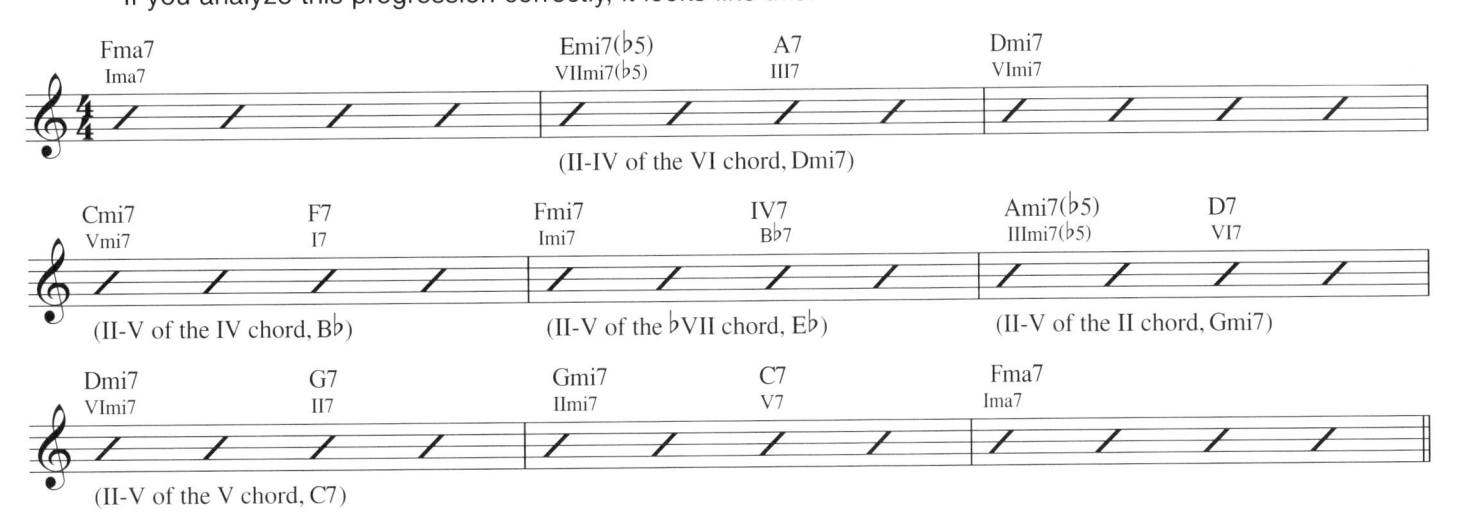

| Fma7 / Ima7 | | Emi7(♭5) / VIImi7(♭5) | A7 / III7 | Dmi7 / VImi7 | |

(II–V of the VI chord, Dmi7)

| Cmi7 / Vmi7 | F7 / I7 | Fmi7 / Imi7 | IV7 / B♭7 | Ami7(♭5) / IIImi7(♭5) | D7 / VI7 |

(II–V of the IV chord, B♭)   (II–V of the ♭VII chord, E♭)   (II–V of the II chord, Gmi7)

| Dmi7 / VImi7 | G7 / II7 | Gmi7 / IImi7 | C7 / V7 | Fma7 / Ima7 | |

(II–V of the V chord, C7)

VIImi7(♭5)–III7 (II–V of VI)

Notice that the Emi7(♭5)–A7 combination actually sets up the VI chord, Dmi7. This is actually a functioning minor II–V–I with the "I" being the VI in the "overall key" of F major.

Vmi7–I7 (II–V of IV)

The Cmi7–F7 combination is a II–V that sets up the IV chord in F, B♭. However, the B♭ is not the next chord. Therefore, the Cmi7–F7 is a non-resolving II–V. (The B♭ does arrive but not until after the Fmi7.)

It's very common to see this chord combination in a jazz standard. This is another typical non-resolving II–V, and therefore the note choice options we've discussed are applicable.

IV7sus–IV7

Notice that the Fmi7–B♭7 is a II–V combination. However, in the key of F (the main key of the song) B♭7 is a IV7 chord. The Fmi7–B♭7 is *not* "setting up" an E♭, which would be the I chord you would expect to follow. B♭7 is simply the IV chord. The Fmi7 acts essentially as a B♭7sus. Why? Analyze the notes of an Fmi7 as if they were over a B♭ root.

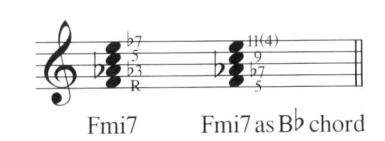

Conclusion? It is very common to see a II–V combination where the dominant chord is actually a IV7 chord in jazz standards. At first glance, an improviser might label this combination as a "II–V," but it can also be regarded as a IV7sus chord followed by a IV7 chord. Regardless of the analysis, we can still treat it as a non-resolving II–V, and therefore the note options we've discussed are applicable.

IIImi7(♭5)–VII7 (minor II–V of II)

Notice that Ami7(♭5)–E7 is a minor II–V combination—a II–V of Gmi, the II chord in the original key of F. However, the Gmi7 is not the next chord. Therefore the Ami7(♭5)–E7 is a non-resolving minor II–V. Locrian ♯2 is a good choice for the Ami7(♭5), while Lydian ♭7 is a good choice for the E7.

VImi7–II7 (II–V of V)

Notice that the Dmi7–G7 combination is a II–V that sets up the V chord in F, C7. However, since the C7 is not the next chord, this is a non-resolving II–V, and the note options we've discussed are applicable.

So we can see that non-resolving II–V progressions occur quite frequently in jazz standards. Regardless of the harmonic analysis, the note choices learned in the first half of this chapter are applicable.

Chapter Summary:

- Non-resolving II–V progressions appear in a number of ways:
  - As IVmi7 to ♭VII7
  - As a truly non-resolving II–V
  - As VIImi7(♭5)–III7 (II–V of VI)
  - As Vmi7–I7 (II–V of IV)
  - As IV7sus7–IV7
  - As IIImi7(♭5)–VII7 (minor II–V of II)
  - As VImi7–II7 (II–V of V)

What we've covered thus far:

- key center and chord tone soloing
- arpeggio organization in major
- arpeggio organization in minor
- common situation concept
- the arpeggio connecting game
- the arpeggio connecting game in more patterns
- expanding our note options with added color tones
- the melodic minor scale
- adding altered tones
- referencing and worksheets
- the connecting game with the altered scale
- the Locrian ♯2 scale
- writing licks
- inserting licks
- disguising licks
- harmonizing the melodic minor scale for altered dominants
- harmonizing the melodic minor scale for minor 7(♭5) chords
- turnaround licks in major (III–VI–II–V–I)
- turnaround licks in minor (I–VI–II–V–I)
- the Lydian ♭7 scale
- harmonizing the melodic minor scale for non-functioning dominants
- non-resolving II–V progressions

What's next:

- the bebop bridge

The Bebop Bridge

Objective:

- To learn to play over the "bebop bridge" (situation #11).

We have now examined the first ten common situations and learned which melodic devices are appropriate for lick building in each. In this chapter we will look at situation #11, a slightly different kind of common situation known as the "bebop bridge." Situation #11 can be seen as a combination of other situations. In fact, there are many expanded common situations that you will begin to recognize as you learn more tunes. Expanded common situations can be thought of as "common combinations" of some of the common situations.

The bebop bridge is a specific set of changes found in many standards with an AABA form. It's sometimes referred to as the B section, or bridge, of these tunes. Tunes like "Scrapple from the Apple," "Anthropology," and "Oleo" all contain this bridge. If you don't prepare in advance, chances are you'll have difficulty playing over this section.

Here's the basic progression:

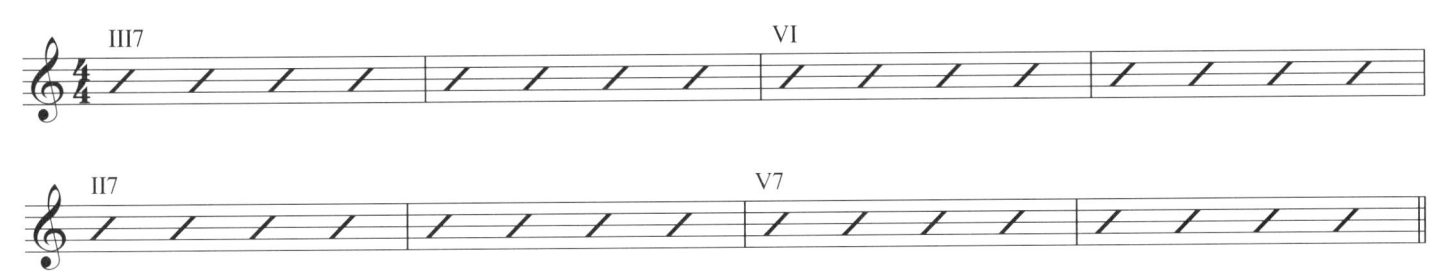

III7		VI7	

II7		V7	

The first thing you should notice is that all of the chords are dominant 7th chords. The III7, VI7, and II7 are all non-diatonic and act as secondary dominants: III7 is V of VI, VI7 is V of II, and II7 is V of V. Let's take a look at this bridge in the context of a song. Here's "Scrapple from the Apple" as an example.

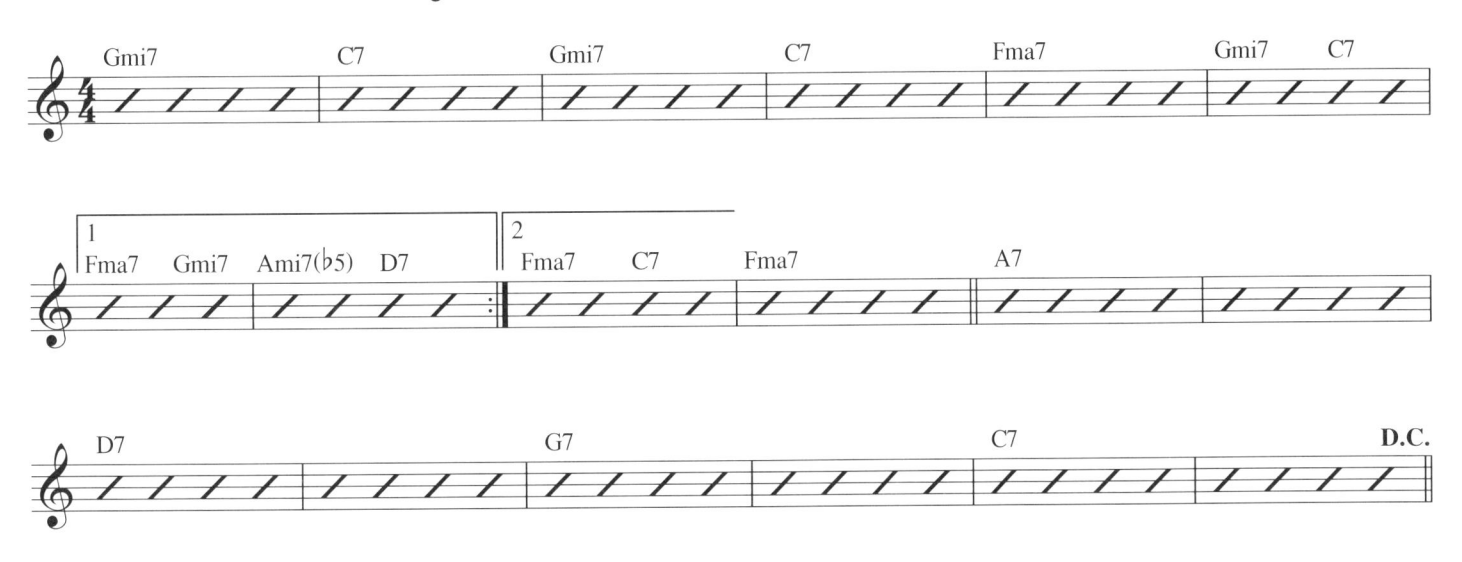

| Gmi7 | C7 | Gmi7 | C7 | Fma7 | Gmi7 C7 |

| 1. Fma7 Gmi7 Ami7(♭5) D7 | 2. Fma7 C7 | Fma7 | A7 |

| D7 | G7 | C7 | D.C. |

"Anthropology" is another good example.

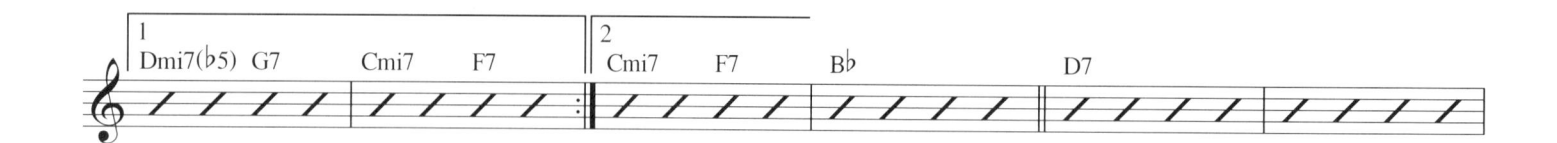

| Bb | G7 | Cmi7 | F7 | Bb | G7 | Cmi7 | F7 | Fmi7 | Bb7 | Ebma7 | Ab7 |

1. | Dmi7(b5) G7 | Cmi7 F7 |
2. | Cmi7 F7 | Bb | D7 |

| G7 | C7 | F7 | D.C. |

Notice that in both of these song examples, the bebop bridge is the B section of an "A-A-B-A" form. The III7 chord at the start of the bridge gives an uplifting change of pace to the progression and separates the bridge from the rest of the song. One obvious note-choice option for the string of dominant 7th chords is to play around the arpeggio of each chord.

A great way to embellish the dominant 7th arpeggio is to use some *chromatic connections*—i.e., connect some specific chord tones with chromatic tones. This idea also works with other chord qualities besides dominant 7th chords and will be addressed in the next chapter.

Let's look at the bebop bridge as it appears in "Scrapple from the Apple," in the key of F.

| A7 | D7 | G7 | C7 |
| III7 | VI7 | II7 | V7 |

Visualize these specific arpeggio shapes to play over the changes.

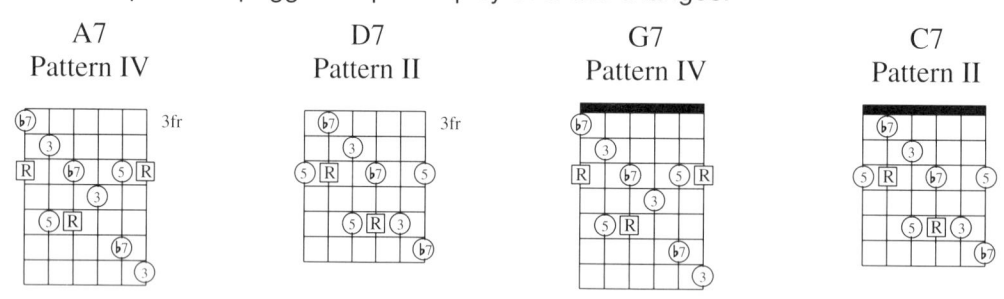

A7 Pattern IV D7 Pattern II G7 Pattern IV C7 Pattern II

If the only notes you use are the dominant 7 chord tones, the improvised melodies you create will be pretty bland. The use of chromatic connections will dress up the sound of the dominant 7th arpeggios while retaining the chord tone sound. The most common chromatic connections on a dominant 7th chord are between the 3rd and the 5th (ascending or descending) and between the root and the b7th (ascending or descending).

Look at this Pattern IV dominant 7th arpeggio.

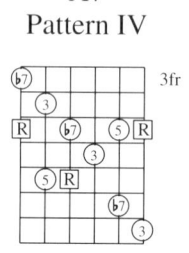

A7 Pattern IV

Chapter 23

Now let's show the chromatic connections between the 3rd and the 5th and between the root and the ♭7th. Listen to the example on the CD demonstrating the use of the chord tones plus the chromatic connections over this shape. You can still hear the sound of the dominant 7th chord, but it doesn't sound as bland.

Track 44

A7
Pattern IV
w/ chromatic connections

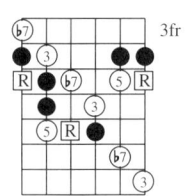

Look at this Pattern II dominant 7th arpeggio.

D7
Pattern II

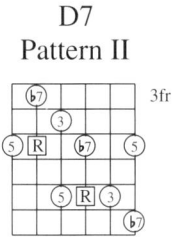

Now here are the chromatic connections between the 3rd and the 5th and between the root and the ♭7th. Listen to the example on the CD demonstrating the use of the chord tones plus the chromatic connections over this shape.

Track 45

D7
Pattern II
w/ chromatic connections

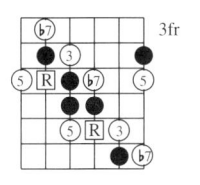

Practice improvising over a static dominant 7th chord to get the feel of using these chromatic connections. you'll find this idea very useful in blues, country, and any other style with dominant 7th chords. Once you are reasonably comfortable using chromatic connections over a static dominant 7th, try stringing them together over the bebop bridge. Here's the progression in the key of F. Try playing over the backing track on the CD using the shapes provided in the diagrams for your lines.

A7 Pattern IV w/ chromatic connections   D7 Pattern II w/ chromatic connections   G7 Pattern IV w/ chromatic connections   C7 Pattern II w/ chromatic connections

Track 46

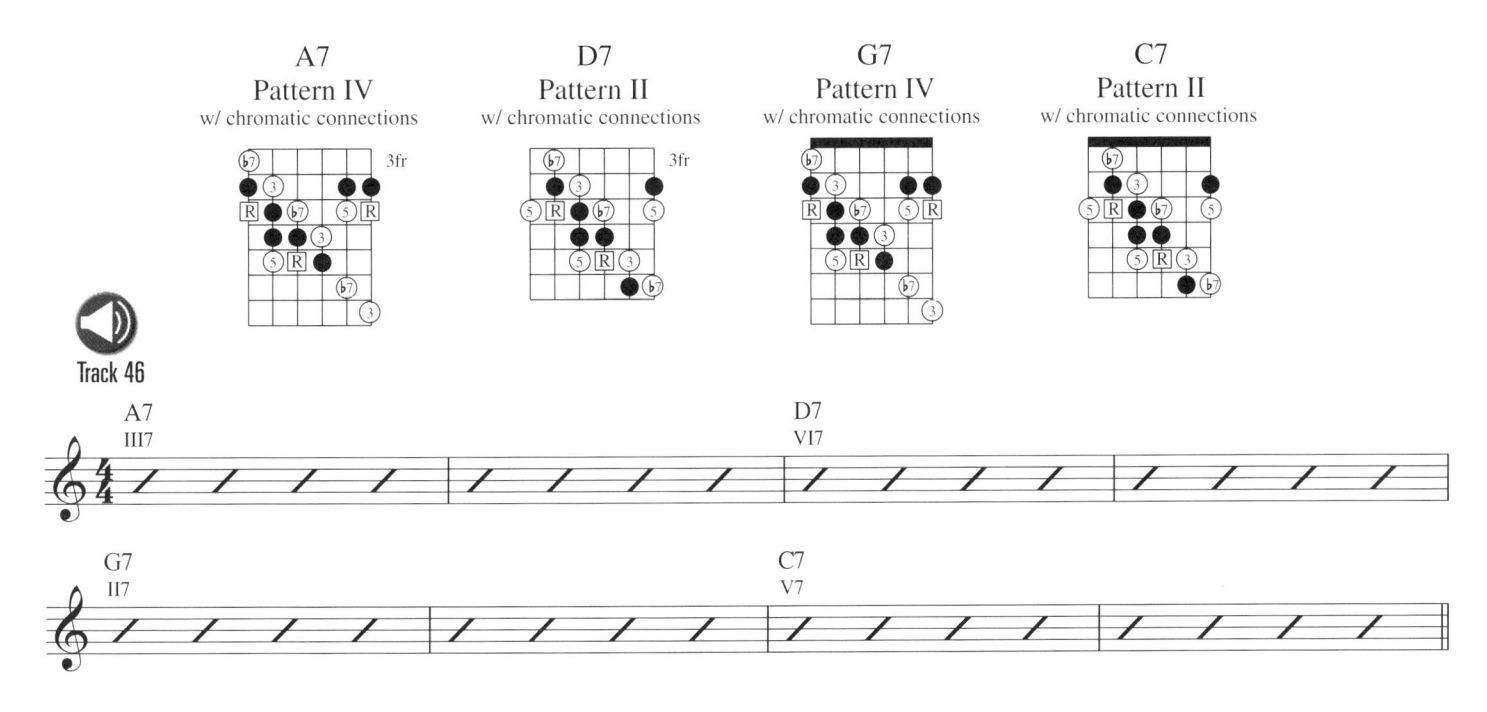

A7 — III7
D7 — VI7
G7 — II7
C7 — V7

Remember that the bebop bridge here is "out of context," meaning that usually you will see this as a B section of an AABA form.

Another set of options allows the improviser to use II–V licks over the bebop bridge by implying chords that are not actually written. This idea of implying chords is not unique to situation #11. However, it provides an ideal opportunity to introduce and demonstrate the concept.

Let's look at the bridge from "Scrapple from the Apple" again. All of the dominant 7th chords are functioning. A7 is V of D7, D7 is V of G7, and G7 is V of C7. As we have seen in situations 1 and 2, II–V progressions are a way of getting back to the I chord. So, what if we placed a mi7 chord (as IImi7) before each of these dominant 7th chords? Let's look a few ways this could be done. Listen to the CD examples of ideas 1, 2, and 3.

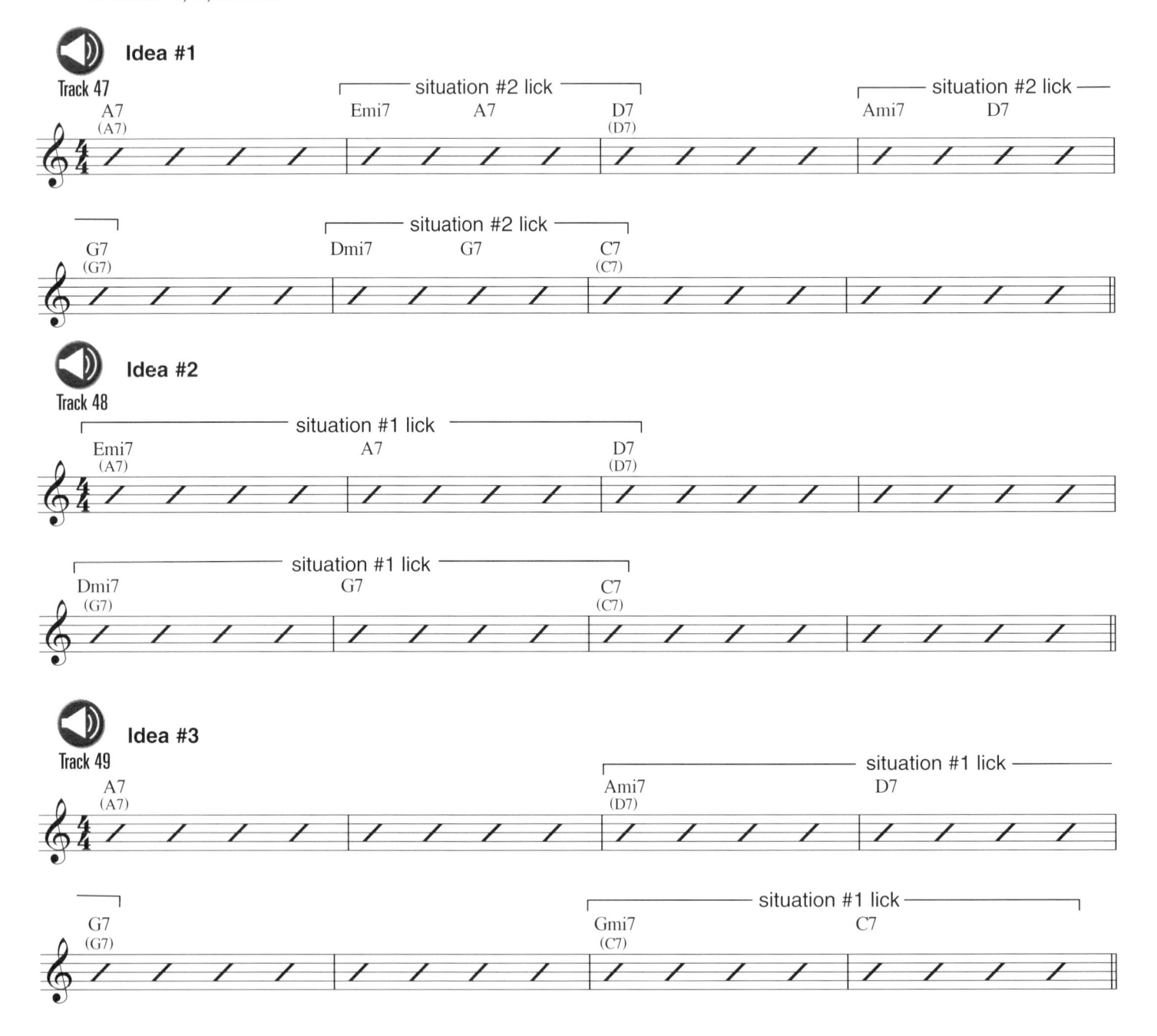

Idea #1

Track 47

| A7 (A7) | Emi7 — situation #2 lick — A7 | D7 (D7) | Ami7 — situation #2 lick — D7 |

| G7 (G7) | Dmi7 — situation #2 lick — G7 | C7 (C7) | |

Idea #2

Track 48

| Emi7 (A7) — situation #1 lick — A7 | | D7 (D7) | |

| Dmi7 (G7) — situation #1 lick — G7 | | C7 (C7) | |

Idea #3

Track 49

| A7 (A7) | | Ami7 (D7) — situation #1 lick — D7 | |

| G7 (G7) | | Gmi7 (C7) — situation #1 lick — C7 | |

Now try playing along with the backing track, inserting long and short II–V licks where appropriate.

Track 50

These are just a few of the ideas you can use for a bebop bridge. You can mix and match these ideas however you want. For example, in Idea #1, you may want to use some of the chromatic connection or Lydian ♭7 ideas on the first measure of the dominant 7th chord before you play the II–V lick.

Chapter 23

Chapter Summary:

- The bebop bridge, situation #11, is common and deserves special attention.
- The first three chords in a bebop bridge (III7, VI7, and II7) are functioning dominants. The V7 is sometimes a functioning dominant chord depending on the tune.
- The chromatic connection approach to playing over dominant 7th chords begins with playing chromatic tones between the 3rd and the 5th (ascending or descending) and between the root and the ♭7th (ascending or descending).
- By implying IImi7 chords before the functioning dominant 7th chords in a bebop bridge, you can make use of your II–V licks.

What we've covered thus far:

- key center and chord tone soloing
- arpeggio organization in major
- arpeggio organization in minor
- common situation concept
- the arpeggio connecting game
- the arpeggio connecting game in more patterns
- expanding our note options with added color tones
- the melodic minor scale
- adding altered tones
- referencing and worksheets
- the connecting game with the altered scale
- the Locrian ♯2 scale
- writing licks
- inserting licks
- disguising licks
- harmonizing the melodic minor scale for altered dominants
- harmonizing the melodic minor scale for minor 7(♭5) chords
- turnaround licks in major (III–VI–II–V–I)
- turnaround licks in minor (I–VI–II–V–I)
- the Lydian ♭7 scale
- harmonizing the melodic minor scale for non-functioning dominants
- non-resolving II–V progressions
- the bebop bridge

What's next:

- chromatic connections

Chromatic Connections

24

Objective:

- To learn to connect chord tones with chromatic tones.

In Chapter 23 we looked at chromatic connections as a way to embellish dominant 7th arpeggios. This was accomplished by connecting some specific chord tones with chromatic tones. This idea works with other chord qualities besides dominant 7th chords as well. Using chromatic connections for major 7, minor 7, and minor 7(b5) chords is just as useful. Let's look at these three remaining diatonic chord qualities separately.

Major 7 Chromatic Connections

The most common chromatic connections on a major 7th chord are between the 3rd and the 5th (ascending or descending) and between the major 7th and major 9th (ascending or descending). Look at these five major 7th arpeggio shapes.

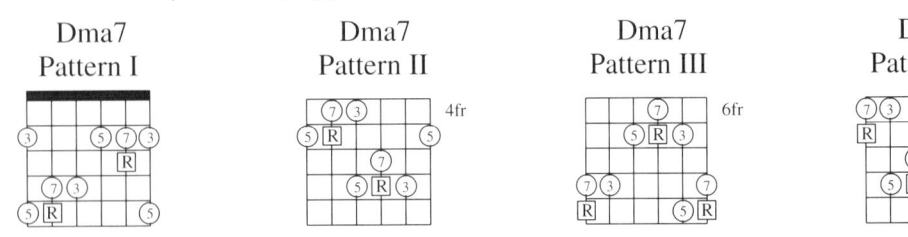

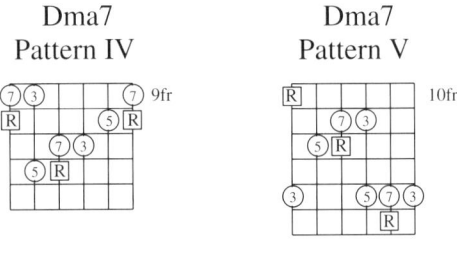

Dma7 Pattern I   Dma7 Pattern II   Dma7 Pattern III   Dma7 Pattern IV   Dma7 Pattern V

Now let's show the chromatic connections between the 3rd and the 5th and between the major 7th and major 9th. Listen to the example on the CD, which demonstrates the use of the chromatic connections over a Dma7 chord.

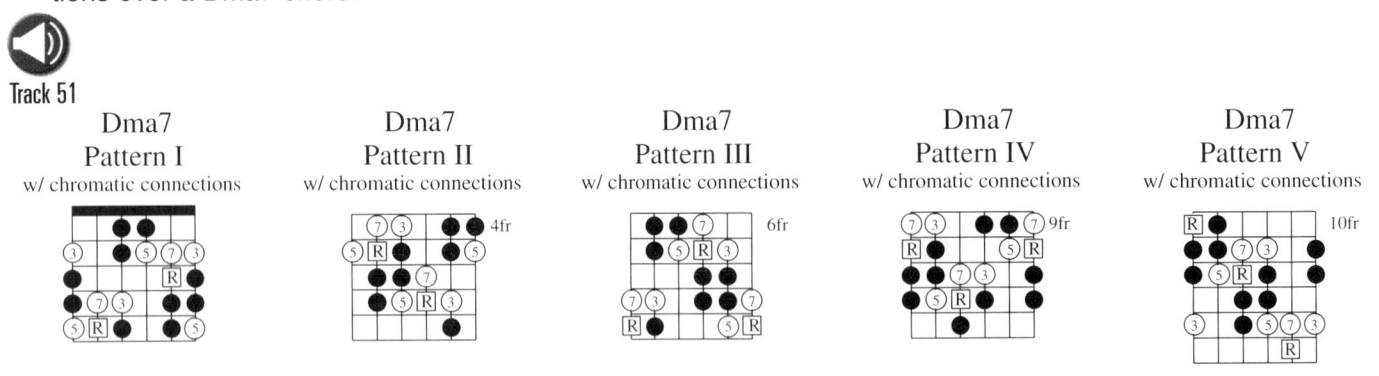

Track 51

Dma7 Pattern I w/ chromatic connections

Dma7 Pattern II w/ chromatic connections

Dma7 Pattern III w/ chromatic connections

Dma7 Pattern IV w/ chromatic connections

Dma7 Pattern V w/ chromatic connections

Practice improvising over a static major 7th chord to get the feel of using these chromatic connections. Once you are reasonably comfortable using chromatic connections over a static major 7th, try using them on the "I part" of a II–V–I lick.

Helpful Hint:

As you become a stronger improviser you'll learn that almost any two chord tones can be connected with chromatic tones. Where the "in between" or chromatic tones lie rhythmically has a lot to do with how well they work. Only through repeated efforts will you become proficient at working these chromatic notes into your playing.

Chapter 24

Minor 7 Chromatic Connections

Minor 7th chords are very accommodating with regard to chromatic connections. In fact, any two chord tones can be connected with chromatic tones. Whichever minor 7th arpeggio shape you are using for improvisation, the idea is the same; wherever you see two chord tones on the same string, there is an opportunity to make a chromatic connection. Look at these five minor 7th arpeggio shapes.

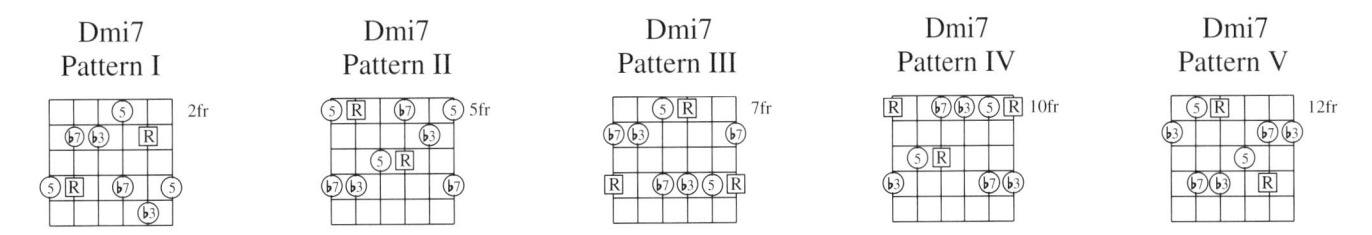

Dmi7 Pattern I Dmi7 Pattern II Dmi7 Pattern III Dmi7 Pattern IV Dmi7 Pattern V

Now let's show the chromatic connections that lie on the same string. It's like filling in the dots between chord tones. Listen to the example on the CD demonstrating the use of the chromatic connections over a Dmi7 chord.

Track 52

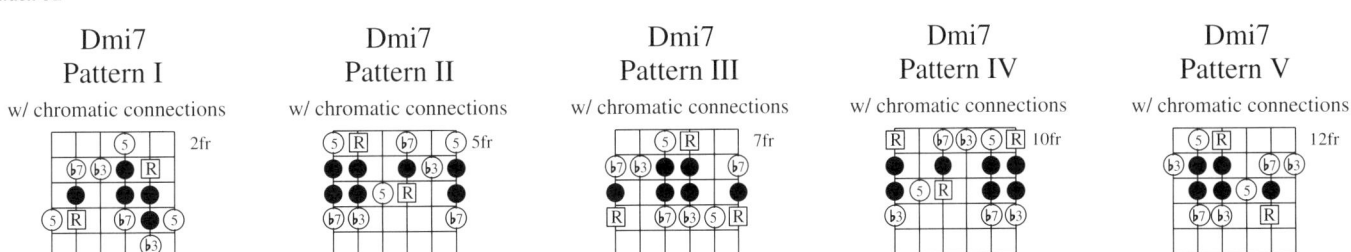

Dmi7 Pattern I w/ chromatic connections
Dmi7 Pattern II w/ chromatic connections
Dmi7 Pattern III w/ chromatic connections
Dmi7 Pattern IV w/ chromatic connections
Dmi7 Pattern V w/ chromatic connections

Practice improvising over a static minor 7th chord to get the feel of using these chromatic connections. Once you are reasonably comfortable using chromatic connections over a static minor 7th, try using them in your lick writing for the "II part" of your major II–V–I licks. You should also use them on "I part" of a minor II–V–I lick.

Minor 7(♭5) Chromatic Connections

Minor 7(♭5) are the same as minor 7 chords with regard to chromatic connections. Wherever you see two chord tones on the same string, there is an opportunity to make a chromatic connection. Look at these five minor 7(♭5) arpeggio shapes.

Dmi7(♭5) Pattern I Dmi7(♭5) Pattern II Dmi7(♭5) Pattern III Dmi7(♭5) Pattern IV Dmi7(♭5) Pattern V

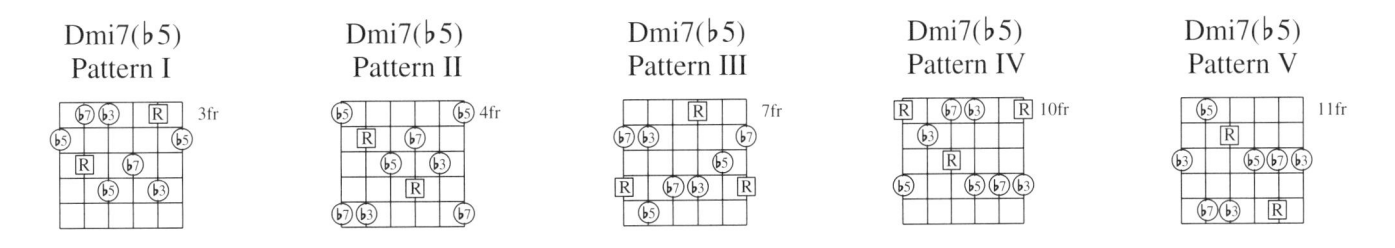

Next let's show the chromatic connections that lie on the same string. Listen to the example on the CD, which demonstrates the use of the chromatic connections over a Dmi7(♭5) chord.

24

Track 53

Dmi7(♭5) Pattern I w/ chromatic connections

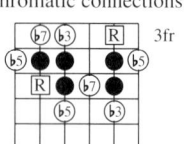

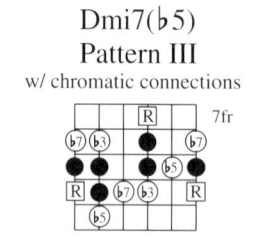

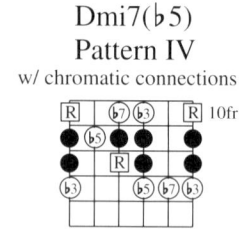

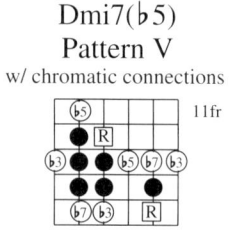

Dmi7(♭5) Pattern II w/ chromatic connections

Dmi7(♭5) Pattern III w/ chromatic connections

Dmi7(♭5) Pattern IV w/ chromatic connections

Dmi7(♭5) Pattern V w/ chromatic connections

Practice improvising over a static minor 7(♭5) chord to get the feel of using these chromatic connections. Once you are reasonably comfortable using chromatic connections over a static minor 7(♭5), try using them in the "II part" of your minor II–V–I licks.

Chapter Summary:

- Using chromatic connections is a way to embellish 7th arpeggios.
- Chromatic connections add color to the use of arpeggios while retaining the chord tone sound and the chord quality.
- As you become a stronger improviser, you'll learn that almost any two chord tones can be connected with chromatic tones.
- Where the chromatic tones lie rhythmically has a lot to do with how well they work.

What we've covered thus far:

- key center and chord tone soloing
- arpeggio organization in major
- arpeggio organization in minor
- common situation concept
- the arpeggio connecting game
- the arpeggio connecting game in more patterns
- expanding our note options with added color tones
- the melodic minor scale
- adding altered tones
- referencing and worksheets
- the connecting game with the altered scale
- the Locrian ♯2 scale
- writing licks
- inserting licks
- disguising licks
- harmonizing the melodic minor scale for altered dominants
- harmonizing the melodic minor scale for minor 7(♭5) chords
- turnaround licks in major (III–VI–II–V–I)
- turnaround licks in minor (I–VI–II–V–I)
- the Lydian ♭7 scale
- harmonizing the melodic minor scale for non-functioning dominants
- non-resolving II–V progressions
- the bebop bridge
- chromatic connections

What's next:

- other melodic devices

25 Other Melodic Devices

Objective:

- To learn other chord tone embellishment methods.

By now you've examined enough songs, written enough licks, and inserted enough licks into to tunes to understand that we need some ideas to play on the chords that don't fall within the bounds of the common situations. This chapter will deal with ideas for the chords that fall "in between" the eleven common situations.

Let's break it down this way. Most of the chords that aren't part of the eleven common situations will be major 7, minor 7, dominant 7, or minor 7(♭5) chords. There are others, but these four chord types are by far the most common. What can you play over these chords? Let's start with the obvious:

- Play in a "key center" approach (improvise with scale tones from the key).
- Play chord tones (arpeggios).
- Play chord tones of the diatonic substitutions (see Chapter 7).
- Play chord tones with chromatic connections (see Chapters 23–24).

These four options are all valid and very useful. Much repetition will enable you to be creative with these techniques, but there's always more to learn. In this chapter we'll study other techniques and devices that will dress up arpeggios.

The Target Phrase

There is one simple idea with many variations that can be applied with great results. It's the idea of "targeting" a strategic note—usually a chord tone or interesting extension—with a series of notes we'll call a *target phrase*. A target phrase is a series of notes leading to a note that you want to be the melodic and rhythmic destination. For example, you may want a phrase to end on the 3rd of an Ami7 chord (C). A target phrase leads you into that C note. The C note is the "destination" of the phrase. You must think of the target note as the destination—both harmonically and rhythmically. Let's look at a few common target phrases.

We'll start with an easy A minor triad shape.

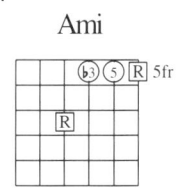

Ami
(♭3)(5)(R) 5fr
(R)

It's obvious now that if the band is playing an A minor chord and we play this arpeggio shape, our line will fit the chord. However, playing only the chord tones is a rather bland sound. Let's invent a few target phrases that will still outline the A minor chord but also embellish the sound.

First, play the A minor shape using only your second finger of your fretting hand. Think of each chord note that your second finger is playing as a target note. This is a preparatory step to show you how you need to think when using target phrases.

When you place your second finger on each chord tone, notice that your first finger lies a half step (one fret) below the target note, and your fourth finger lies a whole step (two frets) above the target note.

Target Phrase 1

The first target phrase we'll learn will start by playing a note one whole step (two frets) above the target note with your fourth finger. We'll then play a note a half step (one fret) below the target note with your first finger. Then we'll play the actual target note. By doing this, you have *encircled* the note.

Now repeat this idea for each tone of the A minor shape. Follow this diagram.

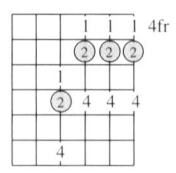

Track 54 Listen to the CD example, which demonstrates over an A minor chord.

Track 55 Now experiment with your own ideas on the play-along track.

Target Phrase 2

Target phrase 2 simply reverses the process of target phrase 1. Here we'll start with our first finger (a half step below the target note). We'll then play a note one whole step (two frets) above the target note. Then we'll play the actual target note with our second finger.

Track 56 Listen to the CD example, which demonstrates over an A minor chord.

Track 57 Now experiment with your own ideas on the play-along track.

Target Phrase 3

The third target phrase we'll learn will be an expansion of target phrase 2. We'll be adding a chromatic note with our third finger in between our fourth finger and the target tone. So we'll be playing three notes before the target tone. See the diagram below. Here we'll start with our first finger (a half step below the target note). We'll then play a note one whole step (two frets) above the target note with our fourth finger. We'll then play a note one half step above the target note with our third finger. Then we'll play the actual target note with our second finger.

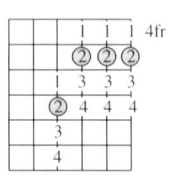

Track 58 Listen to the CD example, which demonstrates over an A minor chord.

Track 59 Now experiment with your own ideas on the play-along track.

Chapter 25

Important:

In the previous examples, we always played the target notes in the same order for the whole arpeggio. We targeted the root, then the 3rd, and then the 5th. That works fine, but you should also try mixing the order of the target notes. For example, you can play a target phrase around the 3rd first, then the root, and then the 5th, etc.

Track 60 🔊 Listen to the CD example, which demonstrates over an A minor chord.

Track 61 🔊 Now experiment with your own ideas on the play-along track.

You can also mix the target phrase types while mixing the order of target notes. For example, you could play target phrase 1 around the 3rd, then target phrase 3 around the root, and then target phrase 2 around the 5th, etc.

Track 62 🔊 Listen to the CD example, which demonstrates over an A minor chord.

Track 63 🔊 Now experiment with your own ideas on the play-along track.

These three target phrases can be adapted for any chord type with some qualifications. Here are the general rules for any chord quality:

- Start with your second finger on the target note.
- Place your first finger one fret below the target note. This note will always work, regardless of whether or not the note is diatonic.
- Normally you only use the note that lies a whole step above the target note when it is diatonic.

As an example, let's create a target phrase 1 for a Cma7 chord. First play the four chord tones of the arpeggio using your second finger. Target phrase 1 calls for us to play a whole step above each target tone followed by a half step below, followed by the target tone. However, we just learned that the note above the target tone should be diatonic. So, we'll need to vary the phrase in order to make this happen. Let's look at how this translates to a Cma7 chord.

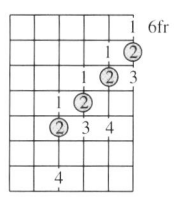

Notice that we altered the pattern for the target notes E and B. This is because the notes that fall one whole step above (F♯ and C♯, respectively) are not diatonic.

Track 64 🔊 Listen to the example on the CD, which demonstrates over a Cma7 chord.

And now try this technique for yourself on the play-along track.

Track 65

Try target phrases with dominant 7th chords, mi7(♭5) chords, and any other chord type you see. Follow the basic rules presented earlier, and you should have no problem.

Chapter Summary:

- After learning to play over the eleven common situations, we need ideas for the chords in between them.
- A target phrase is a series of notes played before a note that you want to be the melodic and rhythmic destination.

What we've covered thus far:

- key center and chord tone soloing
- arpeggio organization in major
- arpeggio organization in minor
- common situation concept
- the arpeggio connecting game
- the arpeggio connecting game in more patterns
- expanding our note options with added color tones
- the melodic minor scale
- adding altered tones
- referencing and worksheets
- the connecting game with the altered scale
- the Locrian ♯2 scale
- writing licks
- inserting licks
- disguising licks
- harmonizing the melodic minor scale for altered dominants
- harmonizing the melodic minor scale for minor 7(♭5) chords
- turnaround licks in major (III–VI–II–V–I)
- turnaround licks in minor (I–VI–II–V–I)
- the Lydian ♭7 scale
- harmonizing the melodic minor scale for non-functioning dominants
- non-resolving II–V progressions
- the bebop bridge
- chromatic connections
- other melodic devices

What's next:

- putting it together

Putting It Together

Objective:

- To learn how to take the lessons learned in this book and put them to work in a long-term plan.

Remember that your job as an improviser can be summarized by two main goals: acquiring repertoire and vocabulary. Let's briefly talk about each.

Repertoire

Your repertoire is the collection of songs you "own." This means you have command of it in several ways. You can:

- play the melody (referred to as the "head")
- solo over the changes
- comp in a duo or group situation

How much repertoire is enough? There's never enough. There are dozens of standards that jazz musicians are expected to know. Start with a goal of ten songs in three to six months. The more tunes you learn, the faster you will learn new ones. The process snowballs once you get ten or more songs in your repertoire.

Vocabulary

Your vocabulary is your collection of licks—written or "borrowed"—from which you base your improvisations. It's made up of the licks you've developed for the eleven common situations as well as the ones you've developed for the chords that lie between or outside the common situations in songs.

Vocabulary can be acquired two ways. You can write your own licks or "borrow" them from other musicians. A side benefit of learning to write licks is that you understand how other musicians created their licks. Chances are a lot of the note choices found in other musicians' licks can be explained in the chapters of this book.

A Learning System

Having a system for building your repertoire and vocabulary takes some of the mystery and anxiety out of the process. Here's a system for organizing yourself as you acquire repertoire while developing and refining your vocabulary. Think of each new song you plan to learn as going through three stages of development.

Stage 1: Learning the Melody, Solo Mapping, and Comping

Melody – In the first stage of working on a song, your first task is to learn the melody (called the "head"). The melody determines the mood of the song. Without knowing the melody, your solos will be without a relevant emotional reference. I suggest that you learn the melody in the pattern where you have the most vocabulary. We have initially developed our licks in Patterns I and III major and Patterns II and IV minor. In your early stages of development, these patterns are the most familiar and should be used as the place to play the melodies. Later as you develop vocabulary for all five major and minor patterns, the pattern you use for the melody becomes less important.

Solo Mapping – "Solo Mapping" a song is the process of analyzing the progression to learn where you will have an opportunity to play the licks you have developed. After the common situations are located, the "in between" chords need to be analyzed, and your melodic options need to be considered and noted. In your early years of development, it's a good idea to actually mark these opportunities on the music. You can even plan and rehearse a specific set of licks and devices so that you can experience a successful pass through the changes. As you gain confidence in your vocabulary, mixing your licks and changing things on the spot becomes easier.

Comping – You need to memorize the chord changes. You'll need to be able to comp in a duo situation where you are the only backing instrument. You'll also need to be able to comp in a band setting with a bass player and drummer.

Stage 2: Repetition

There is no substitute for repetition! As improvisers, we are looking for the freedom to play what our minds imagine. Remember these four statements:

1. Repetition creates familiarity.
2. Familiarity builds confidence.
3. Confidence brings freedom.
4. Freedom allows you to play what you hear.

There is no other way to get good at this. You must invest the time in this stage. Stage 2 is the process of taking the preparatory steps from Stage 1 and repeating them regularly. There is no way to gauge when you're ready for stage 3. You will be playing a song for the thousandth time and find yourself feeling very confident and comfortable, stretching for ideas you've never played before. You'll have a realization: "Hey! I can do this."

As a beginner, songs that you've learned in Stage 1 will need to spend weeks or months in Stage 2. Later you'll be able to move songs through stages more quickly as you learn more songs.

Stage 3: Improvise with Your Vocabulary

Once you get a song through Stage 2, you are ready to begin really playing music. Up until now, our study and practice has been about technical concepts. We've been very scientific about how to select notes for each chord and common situation. In Chapter 13 we learned to write licks. How do we get beyond repeating our rehearsed licks in Stage 2? Typically, a guitarist who has been disciplined about doing the repetitions required in Stage 2 will simply "fall into" Stage 3. The lick that has been repeated hundreds of times will evolve into a new lick perhaps by accident, design, or some spontaneous inspiration. The only way this is achieved is through repetition.

Once a song is "owned," a daily performance of it should not focus on repeating the licks note-for-note, but on taking chances with new lines and licks conceived spontaneously. The work done in Stage 2 shows your ears, eyes, and fingers where to go. Don't expect your harmonic sound to be different from your licks. Your licks taught you the sounds of the devices and options. The difference will be that now you have the freedom to go where you want, when you want.

It's a good idea to keep track of your repertoire with a list. Make a column for each stage. You should only have one song in the Stage 1 column at a time. You can have one or two in Stage 2. It's a lot of fun to watch the Stage 3 column grow!

Chapter 26

Chapter Summary:

- Your main focus is to acquire vocabulary and repertoire.
- To "own" a song means that from memory you can play the melody, solo over the changes, and comp in a duo or group situation.

What we've covered thus far:

- key center and chord tone soloing
- arpeggio organization in major
- arpeggio organization in minor
- common situation concept
- the arpeggio connecting game
- the arpeggio connecting game in more patterns
- expanding our note options with added color tones
- the melodic minor scale
- adding altered tones
- referencing and worksheets
- the connecting game with the altered scale
- the Locrian ♯2 scale
- writing licks
- inserting licks
- disguising licks
- harmonizing the melodic minor scale for altered dominants
- harmonizing the melodic minor scale for minor 7(♭5) chords
- turnaround licks in major (III–VI–II–V–I)
- turnaround licks in minor (I–VI–II–V–I)
- the Lydian ♭7 scale
- harmonizing the melodic minor scale for non-functioning dominants
- non-resolving II–V progressions
- the bebop bridge
- chromatic connections
- other melodic devices
- putting it together

What's next:

- solo shaping

Solo Shaping

27

> **Objective:**
>
> - To learn about the compositional element of soloing.

After hearing literally thousands of guitar players play solos of varying levels of quality in my years teaching at GIT, my ear has focused on several things that make a solo a memorable event. Good time, feel, note choice, and tone are all important, but there is another equally important element: *shape*.

This is a topic left out of many guitar related discussions, how-to books, seminars, and programs. To clarify "solo shaping," let's use this analogy. A solo is really a story you are telling on your guitar to a listener. Stories of all kinds (books, movies, TV shows) all share common elements: a beginning, a middle, and an end. We certainly wouldn't want to hear a storyteller put together a bunch of unrelated sentences and paragraphs. Instead, we expect to be introduced to the theme of the story, then taken through some interesting twists and turns, and then brought to a satisfying conclusion that is clear and definite.

Too many times guitarists play solos that are collections of unrelated licks and noodlings that, for a brief minute, could be ear-catching because of their speed, complexity, or volume. A second listening to the same solo, however, might leave you less than satisfied.

This book has taught you how to write those licks. However, you need to evolve beyond the point of stringing licks together. You need to evolve into an improviser who takes the use of their vocabulary to the next level. Your licks teach your ear, mind, and fingers what the notes on the guitar sound like. The next level is to use your licks as "finger paths."

When I think of all the truly great solos played on guitar (or any instrument for that matter), the one element always present is shape. It's the pacing of intensity of the solo. You need to focus on solo shaping when you move a song into Stage 3. There are many shapes or contours to which you can mold a solo. Here are a few that are common:

1. Start at low intensity and build to peak at the very end.
2. Start at low intensity and build to peak near the end then float the listener down in the last few measures.
3. Begin at a very intense level, drop it down and then gradually build to the end.

These are just a few, but the possibilities are endless. A couple of factors sometimes predetermine the shape of a solo:

Length: If you've only got eight measures, you can't waste any time getting to the point. At the other extreme, an open-ended solo allows you the luxury of developing ideas gradually over a long period of time. This is really "slow cooking." Long solos allow you to bring the listener up and down several times if you've got enough interesting ideas to develop.

Setting: This deals with what precedes the solo and what comes after it. If you have a solo that follows a vocal section, you may need to start the solo at the same intensity level the singer ended with. Likewise, you may need to deliver the listener back to the level of intensity of the vocal entrance at the end of your solo.

Here's an experiment for the classic solo shape. The solo starts at a low intensity and peaks at the end. Think of the following ideas as ways to contrast and build your solo from beginning to end. Start low, slow, sparse, simple, and soft. End your solo high, fast, with lots of notes, complicated, and loud. If you contrast any two or more of these elements, your solo will begin to have shape.

Low	>	High
Slow	>	Fast
Sparse	>	Dense (lots of notes)
Simple	>	Complex
Soft	>	Loud

Use this simple four-measure progression that you can solo on in one key (key center and/or licks). Record the progression playing rhythm guitar so you can play over it.

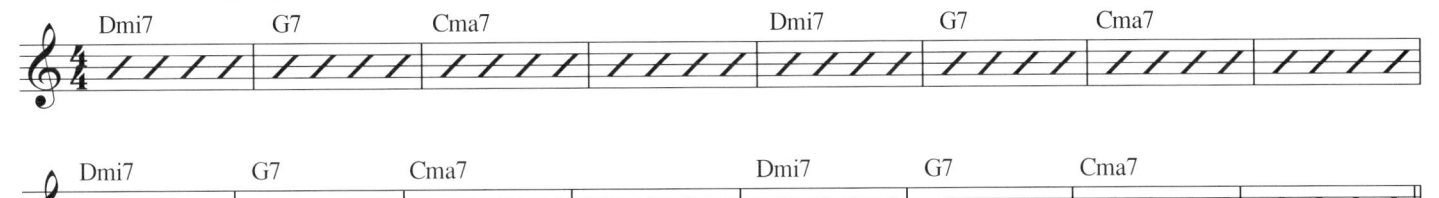

Think of your solo as having "four periods" like a basketball game. In the first period play a simple three- or four-note idea in a middle register of your guitar. Don't be afraid to leave lots of space. In the second period, repeat the first idea almost note-for-note. You've now played a "theme" that the listener can relate to since they've heard it twice. In the third period, move up to a higher register and play either a brand new idea or a more complicated version of the original idea. In the forth period, play something even higher with more notes that resembles your third-period idea.

Of course this is a very simple version of a "shaped" solo, but it does get you started thinking the right way. Practice this concept daily.

When you feel are ready, expand the exercise. Double the length of the above progression. Now think of your solo as having eight periods. You might approach this new longer solo like this:

1. In the first period play a simple three- or four-note idea in a middle register of your guitar. Don't be afraid to leave lots of space.
2. In the second period, repeat the first idea almost note-for-note. You've now played a "theme" that the listener can relate to since they've heard it twice.
3. In the third period, move up to a higher register and play either a brand new idea or a more complicated version of the original idea.
4. In the fourth period, mimic the idea you played in the third period. You are at the halfway point of your solo.
5. In the fifth period, play a new idea in the same general register as the fourth period idea. This can be an expansion of one of the earlier ideas or a completely new statement.
6. In the sixth period, repeat the fifth period idea.
7. In the seventh period, build on the fifth and sixth period idea with more notes, stronger intensity, and a higher register.
8. In the eighth and final period, play a strong melodic and rhythmic statement with a very definite ending.

Applying this concept is more difficult in more complex songs. The progression above is very simple and repetitive. The harmony in real jazz standards is usually quite more complicated. To apply the solo shaping idea over a song with an AABA form or any other form requires real command of your vocabulary. The build from low to high, slow to fast, sparse to dense, simple to complex, and soft to loud is possible in any song. It just requires more command of vocabulary, more concentration, and more practice.

Whether you are playing a simple or complex song, your solo needs to have a shape. The listener shouldn't be able to tell the difference between a harmonically simple or complex song by what they hear you play. They should feel as though they've been told a good story.

Chapter Summary:

- A solo is a story you are telling on your guitar to a listener.
- Stories of all kinds share common elements: a beginning, middle, and end.
- The following list shows the elements of contrast that will give a solo shape:

Low	>	High
Slow	>	Fast
Sparse	>	Dense (lots of notes)
Simple	>	Complex
Soft	>	Loud

What we've covered thus far:

- key center and chord tone soloing
- arpeggio organization in major
- arpeggio organization in minor
- common situation concept
- the arpeggio connecting game
- the arpeggio connecting game in more patterns
- expanding our note options with added color tones
- the melodic minor scale
- adding altered tones
- referencing and worksheets
- the connecting game with the altered scale
- the Locrian ♯2 scale
- writing licks
- inserting licks
- disguising licks
- harmonizing the melodic minor scale for altered dominants
- harmonizing the melodic minor scale for minor 7(♭5) chords
- turnaround licks in major (III–VI–II–V–I)
- turnaround licks in minor (I–VI–II–V–I)
- the Lydian ♭7 scale
- harmonizing the melodic minor scale for non-functioning dominants
- non-resolving II–V progressions
- the bebop bridge
- chromatic connections
- other melodic devices
- putting it together
- solo shaping

What's next:

- how to budget practice time

How to Budget Practice Time

> **Objective:**
>
> - To learn how to practice efficiently.

Time is precious. Wasting time practicing the wrong things doesn't make sense. There are more self-taught guitar players than any other kind of instrumentalists. Having had no teacher to guide us in our practice, most of us have no idea about how to organize our time. This chapter will present a simple method to help organize your time—not only with the materials in this book, but with all materials you need to practice.

Compare your physical and mental development as a guitarist to a body-builder. A body-builder will focus on a specific exercise for each specific muscle in a very organized way. They plan out the days, the number of repetitions, and the amount of time they will devote to each exercise. The key here is consistency. The routine of repeating the exercise regularly and in the appropriate amounts enables the proper and healthy building of muscles. The exact same thing can be said about learning to play an instrument. If you put off practice until Saturday and then practice too many hours, you could suffer physically and you will probably not develop mentally as fast as you could with a more balanced and steady practice routine.

Technique

Technique is the physical act of playing the instrument. Although it is important, guitarists can easily over-practice technique. Exercises like sequences are great for building muscle, learning coordination, and developing a "touch." Remember, guitarists work on muscles too—the small ones in the hands and fingers. The same "big muscle" rules about stretching, rest, and pacing apply to working with the muscles in your hands and fingers.

Stretching

Before practicing, spend a few minutes gently stretching your fingers back and apart. Be careful! These are small muscles. You can hurt yourself if you stretch too far. You can even stretch when you are not getting ready to practice.

Ten to twenty slow and perfectly executed repetitions is adequate when you are learning something brand new. The key is in the regularity and the routine discussed in the next paragraph. After an exercise is learned, the number of repetitions can be reduced to two or three because at this point, you are only maintaining your ability to execute the exercise.

Routine

The key to a body builder's success is in the routine they maintain. They might work on their upper body Monday, Wednesday, and Friday and their lower body Tuesday, Thursday, and Saturday. The day off between workouts of the upper or lower body allows the muscle to rest and rebuild. The regularity of the routine enables progress to be made over time.

Apply this philosophy of regularity to your technique and creative practice. Start by making a detailed list of all of your technique, creative, and vocabulary/song learning objectives. List each exercise separately by scale or arpeggio pattern so that each specific exercise has an entry on your list. Your routine is like a "to do" list. If it's written down on paper, you will develop a sense of obligation to the routine you've designed for yourself. I suggest you design your routine on a day that you have a clear mind. That way later in the week when life has scrambled your brains a little, you can trust the person (you) who designed the routine with a clear head.

Take your detailed list of things you want to practice and assign them to "time compartments." You might only allow two or three minutes for an exercise. What is always hard to accept is that a few good repetitions over a period of days and weeks is better than many repetitions for a long period of time in one sitting.

Update your routine periodically. Every couple of weeks you should review the way you are budgeting your time. This can be a time to consolidate some exercises that have become easy for you into shorter "maintenance" routines, allowing more time for you to learn new things. It is very easy for guitarists to fall into the habit of practicing the same exact exercises for months or years because it makes them feel secure in their playing. I recommend taking already-learned material and consolidating it into a few fifteen- or thirty-minute warm-up routines that can be alternated as such:

Monday	routine 1
Tuesday	routine 2
Wednesday	routine 3
Thursday	routine 1
Friday	routine 2
Saturday	routine 3
Sunday	day off

I also recommend building creative time into your schedule. Remember why you picked up the guitar in the first place? You liked to play it. It was fun. The sound was appealing. Don't lose sight of your innocent attraction to music and the instrument. To become proficient at anything, you need to dedicate long and hard hours of practice which can make you lose your perspective. Don't let the hard work spoil your child-like fascination with music. Don't let your guitar become a beast that demands your time. This is called *burnout*. Budgeting creative time into your daily practice routine is the best defense against burnout. If you have two hours a day to practice, you could divide it up as follows:

technique	30 minutes
vocabulary	30 minutes
repertoire	30 minutes
creative "free play"	30 minutes

This, of course, is a very crude example, but it gives you some perspective. The main point is that you need to be organized and disciplined but still make practicing fun.

Conclusion

You have now reached the base of the mountain. Keep the following in mind:

- Continue your work toward executing the connecting game in all five major and minor scale patterns. Remember to include the "color tone" alternatives (diatonic subs, altered, etc.).
- Continue your work toward developing vocabulary in all five major and minor scale patterns.
- Continue inserting and disguising your licks until you are so familiar with them that you feel free to change them spontaneously.
- Continue learning to shape a solo (tell a story) so that your listener feels they've been somewhere with you.
- Continue to build vocabulary and repertoire.
- Listen to jazz and all other kinds of music. Find the great improvisers and transcribe.

Good luck, and practice, practice, practice!

Musicians Institute Press

is the official series of Southern California's renowned music school, Musicians Institute. **MI** instructors, some of the finest musicians in the world, share their vast knowledge and experience with you – no matter what your current level. For guitar, bass, drums, vocals, and keyboards, **MI Press** offers the finest music curriculum for higher learning through a variety of series:

ESSENTIAL CONCEPTS
Designed from MI core curriculum programs.

MASTER CLASS
Designed from MI elective courses.

PRIVATE LESSONS
Tackle a variety of topics "one-on-one" with MI faculty instructors.

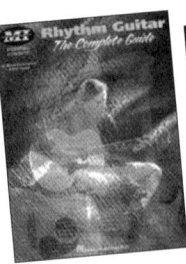

BASS

Arpeggios for Bass
by Dave Keif • Private Lessons
00695133 .... $12.95

The Art of Walking Bass
by Bob Magnusson • Master Class
00695168 Book/CD Pack................ $17.95

Bass Fretboard Basics
by Paul Farnen • Essential Concepts
00695201 .... $14.95

Bass Playing Techniques
by Alexis Sklarevski • Essential Concepts
00695207 .... $16.95

Grooves for Electric Bass
by David Keif • Private Lessons
00695265 Book/CD Pack................ $14.95

Latin Bass
by George Lopez and David Keif • Private Lessons
00695543 Book/CD Pack................ $14.95

Music Reading for Bass
by Wendy Wrehovcsik • Essential Concepts
00695203 .... $10.95

Odd-Meter Bassics
by Dino Monoxelos • Private Lessons
00695170 Book/CD Pack................ $14.95

GUITAR

Advanced Guitar Soloing
by Daniel Gilbert & Beth Marlis • Essential Concepts
00695636 Book/CD Pack................ $19.95

Advanced Scale Concepts & Licks for Guitar
by Jean Marc Belkadi • Private Lessons
00695298 Book/CD Pack $14.95

Basic Blues Guitar
by Steve Trovato • Private Lessons
00695180 Book/CD Pack $14.95

Blues/Rock Soloing for Guitar
by Robert Calva • Private Lessons
00695680 Book/CD Pack $17.95

Chord Progressions for Guitar
by Tom Kolb • Private Lessons
00695664 Book/CD Pack $14.95

Classical & Fingerstyle Guitar Techniques
by David Oakes • Master Class
00695171 Book/CD Pack................ $14.95

Contemporary Acoustic Guitar
by Eric Paschal & Steve Trovato • Master Class
00695320 Book/CD Pack................ $16.95

Creative Chord Shapes
by Jamie Findlay • Private Lessons
00695172 Book/CD Pack................ $9.95

Diminished Scale for Guitar
by Jean Marc Belkadi • Private Lessons
00695227 Book/CD Pack................ $9.95

Essential Rhythm Guitar
by Steve Trovato • Private Lessons
00695181 Book/CD Pack................ $14.95

Funk Guitar
by Ross Bolton • Private Lessons
00695419 Book/CD Pack................ $14.95

Guitar Basics
by Bruce Buckingham • Private Lessons
00695134 Book/CD Pack................ $16.95

Guitar Fretboard Workbook
by Barrett Tagliarino • Essential Concepts
00695712 .... $14.95

Guitar Hanon
by Peter Deneff • Private Lessons
00695321 .... $9.95

Guitar Lick•tionary
by Dave Hill • Private Lessons
00695482 Book/CD Pack................ $17.95

Guitar Soloing
by Dan Gilbert & Beth Marlis • Essential Concepts
00695190 Book/CD Pack................ $19.95
00695638 VHS Video..................... $19.95

Harmonics for Guitar
by Jamie Findlay • Private Lessons
00695169 Book/CD Pack................ $9.95

Jazz Guitar Chord System
by Scott Henderson • Private Lessons
00695291 .... $9.95

Jazz Guitar Improvisation
by Sid Jacobs • Master Class
00695128 Book/CD Pack................ $17.95
00695639 VHS Video..................... $19.95

Jazz-Rock Triad Improvising
by Jean Marc Belkadi • Private Lessons
00695361 Book/CD Pack................ $14.95

Latin Guitar
by Bruce Buckingham • Master Class
00695379 Book/CD Pack................ $14.95

Modern Approach to Jazz, Rock & Fusion Guitar
by Jean Marc Belkadi • Private Lessons
00695143 Book/CD Pack................ $14.95

Modern Jazz Concepts for Guitar
by Sid Jacobs • Master Class
00695711 Book/CD Pack................ $16.95

Modern Rock Rhythm Guitar
by Danny Gill • Private Lessons
00695682 Book/CD Pack................ $14.95

Modes for Guitar
by Tom Kolb • Private Lessons
00695555 Book/CD Pack................ $16.95

Music Reading for Guitar
by David Oakes • Essential Concepts
00695192 .... $16.95

The Musician's Guide to Recording Acoustic Guitar
by Dallan Beck • Private Lessons
00695505 Book/CD Pack................ $12.95

The Musician's Guide to Recording Drums
by Dallan Beck • Private Lessons
00695755 Book/CD Pack................ $19.95

Outside Guitar Licks
by Jean Marc Belkadi • Private Lessons
00695697 Book/CD Pack................ $14.95

Practice Trax for Guitar
by Danny Gill • Private Lessons
00695601 Book/CD Pack................ $14.95

Progressive Tapping Licks
by Jean Marc Belkadi • Private Lessons
00695748 Book/CD Pack................ $14.95

Rhythm Guitar
by Bruce Buckingham & Eric Paschal • Essential Concepts
00695188 Book............................ $16.95
00695644 VHS Video..................... $19.95

Rock Lead Basics
by Nick Nolan & Danny Gill • Master Class
00695144 Book/CD Pack................ $15.95
00695637 VHS Video..................... $19.95

Rock Lead Performance
by Nick Nolan & Danny Gill • Master Class
00695278 Book/CD Pack................ $16.95

Rock Lead Techniques
by Nick Nolan & Danny Gill • Master Class
00695146 Book/CD Pack................ $15.95

Slap & Pop Technique for Guitar
00695645 Book/CD Pack................ $12.95

Texas Blues Guitar
by Robert Calva • Private Lessons
00695340 Book/CD Pack................ $16.95

Prices, contents, and availability subject to change without notice

FOR MORE INFORMATION, SEE YOUR LOCAL MUSIC DEALER, OR WRITE TO:

HAL•LEONARD® CORPORATION
7777 W. BLUEMOUND RD. P.O. BOX 13819 MILWAUKEE, WI 53213
Visit Hal Leonard Online at **www.halleonard.com**

0604